BEHOLD MY PRESENT TESTAMENT,

THE CONTINUANCE OF MY OLD AND NEW TESTAMENT,
SAYS THE LORD GOD
"VOLUMES THIRTY-THREE AND THIRTY-FOUR"

"BEHOLD THE LAMB OF GOD"
CHRIST JESUS, THE HOLY LAMB OF GOD

BY:
BARBARA ANN MARY MACK

AuthorHouse™
1663 Liberty Drive
Bloomington, IN 47403
www.authorhouse.com
Phone: 1 (800) 839-8640

© 2019 BARBARA ANN MARY MACK. All rights reserved.

No part of this book may be reproduced, stored in a retrieval system, or transmitted by any means without the written permission of the author.

Published by AuthorHouse 04/11/2019

ISBN: 978-1-7283-0758-9 (hc)
ISBN: 978-1-7283-0756-5 (sc)
ISBN: 978-1-7283-0757-2 (e)

Print information available on the last page.

This book is printed on acid-free paper.

Because of the dynamic nature of the Internet, any web addresses or links contained in this book may have changed since publication and may no longer be valid. The views expressed in this work are solely those of the author and do not necessarily reflect the views of the publisher, and the publisher hereby disclaims any responsibility for them.

CONTENTS

DEDICATION 1
ACKNOWLEDGMENT 4
PROLOGUE 5
BEHOLD MY PRESENT TESTAMENT - VOLUME THIRTY-THREE 9
BEHOLD MY PRESENT TESTAMENT – VOLUME THIRTY-FOUR 155
EPILOGUE 180
MY OTHER PUBLISHED BOOKS 182

DEDICATION

TO: *CHRIST JESUS,* THE LAMB OF GOD, OUR FATHER, AND KENNETH AND CHARLENE CARLISLE, OWNERS OF **LITTLE HOOVES ROMNEYS FARM.**

A DIVINE MESSAGE FROM ALMIGHTY GOD TO HIS BLESSED SON AND DAUGHTER, KENNETH, AND HIS LOVELY WIFE CHARLENE. FOR THEY OPENED THEIR HEARTS AND FARM TO *BARBARA,* THE LORD'S HEAVEN SENT MESSENGER TODAY.

To: Blessed Charlene and Kenneth

Barbara Ann Mary Mack

May 7, 2019

KENNETH, *MY BLESSED SON*

ALMIGHTY GOD SPEAKING TO KENNETH CARLISLE

MY SON-

O BLESSED *CHOSEN ONE*-
CONTINUE IN *MY LOVE*-
AS YOU ENJOY THE BEAUTY THAT DESCENDS FROM *SWEET HEAVEN ABOVE.*
CLING TO ME-
THROUGH THE REALM OF *SWEET ETERNITY.*
FOR *BLESSED AND TRUE*-
IS THE HOLY GOD WHO FORMED *YOUR LOVELY FAMILY AND YOU.*
WALK WITH ME, *O BELOVED ONE.*
CLING TO MY MERCY AND GRACE, *O WORTHY AND BLESSED SON.*
MARCH 30, 2019

MY BEAUTIFUL DAUGHTER, *CHARLENE*

ALMIGHTY GOD SPEAKING TO CHARLENE CARLISLE

MY LOVELY DAUGHTER: I HAVE GIVEN AND BLESSED YOU WITH THE GIFT OF A VERY CARING AND KIND HEART. CONTINUE IN MY LOVE, *DEAR DAUGHTER OF MINE*-
FOR I WILL TREASURE YOUR BEAUTY AND PRESENCE THROUGHOUT *THE REALM OF UNENDING TIME.*
FOR *HOLY AND TRUE*-
IS THE LOVE THAT YOUR HEAVENLY FATHER AND GOD HAVE FOR *BELOVED YOU.*
MARCH 30, 2019

ACKNOWLEDGMENT

The sovereignty of *Christ Jesus* has been proclaimed throughout the lands. Let every believing voice unite in praise- *Hallelujah! Hallelujah! Hallelujah* to *Christ Jesus,* the sovereign king of kings! *Hallelujah! Hallelujah, to Christ Jesus,* the victorious sacrificial lamb of God.

All farm animals images and photos are courtesy of Kenneth and Charlene Carlisle, owners of Little Hooves Romneys Farm, located in Moorsetown, New Jersy

On April 1, 2019, the Lord God led me to the Little Hooves Romneys Farm, located in Moorestown, New Jersey. During our tour, we were permitted to take photos of the lambs and sheep, so that I may include them in my book. The owners of the farm, Kenneth & Charlene Carlisle, were very friendly and kind. I felt like we were old friends. The lambs and sheep were friendly as well. I was able to hold a couple of the baby lambs and bottle feed one of them. I really enjoyed this God given blessing. May almighty God continue sending down his many blessings to Charlene, Kenneth, and their loved ones.

PROLOGUE

CHRIST JESUS, THE LAMB OF GOD, SPEAKING

IN THE BEGINNING: YES, THE VERY BEGINNING, I, THE LORD JESUS CHRIST, WALKED IN THE MIDST OF GOD, THE FATHER. FOR, I ALONE, WAS BEGOTTEN BY THE FATHER. I WAS NOT CREATED FROM THE DUST OF THE GROUND AS MANKIND WAS FORMED.

IN THE BEGINNING: I EXISTED WITH GOD, THE FATHER- YES, THE *DIVINE ONE*; MY DIVINE ORIGIN; MY DIVINE HOME.

IN THE BEGINNING; I, THE LORD JESUS, YES, CHRIST JESUS, THE FORETOLD *MESSIAH*-YES, THE *SACRIFICIAL LAMB OF GOD, THE FATHER;* MY DIVINE ORIGIN. YES, THE DIVINE HOLY ONE *(ALMIGHTY GOD, THE FATHER)* WHO *BEGAT ME ALONE.*

IN THE BEGINNING: I WALKED IN THE ESSENCE OF GOD, OUR HEAVENLY FATHER, AS HE AND I FUSED IN THE MIDST OF *DIVINITY,* AND CREATED HUMAN BEINGS AND EVERY LIVING FORM ON, AND BENEATH THE LANDS AND THE WATERS. HUMAN BEINGS WERE CREATED FOR ME AND BY ME; WHO IS *ALMIGHTY GOD, THE SON; THE DIVINE ONE.*

IN THE BEGINNING: THE FATHER AND I SAW THAT EVERYTHING THAT WAS FORMED BY GOD, THE FATHER, AND ME, WAS VERY GOOD.
BUT THAT CHANGED BECAUSE OF DISOBEDIENCE. THEREFORE, I, *CHRIST JESUS,* THE FORETOLD *MESSIAH AND GOD;* THE FORETOLD *KING OF KINGS;* THE FORETOLD *SACRIFICIAL LAMB OF GOD,* WAS SENT IN THE FORM OF FLESH, *IN THE FORM OF MAN,* TO REPAIR AND *MAKE RIGHT* THAT WHICH WAS MADE IMPERFECT BY MANKIND.

IN THE BEGINNING: GOD, OUR FATHER, AND I, DISCUSSED WHAT NEED TO BE DONE IN ORDER TO SAVE MANKIND FROM TOTAL DESTRUCTION. IN TOTAL AGREEMENT WITH THE FATHER, I WAS SENT, BY HIM, BECAUSE I ALONE, COULD MAKE THINGS RIGHT IN THE PRESENCE OF THE FATHER. WE DISCUSSED THE NATURE AND DEPTH OF *MY DIVINE ASSIGNMENT OF LOVE.* I ALONE, AM PURE ENOUGH TO BE A SACRIFICE FOR OUR (GOD, THE FATHER AND GOD, THE SON) CHILDREN ON EARTH. *I AM THE ONLY ESSENCE OF DIVINITY* WHO COULD BRING MANKIND AND US TOGETHER AGAIN. *HOLY IS HE* (ALMIGHTY GOD, THE FATHER) WHO SENT **UNBLEMISHED** (WITHOUT SIN OR CORRUPTION) *ME- YES, THE SACRIFICIAL LAMB OF GOD ALMIGHTY.*

BEHOLD MY PRESENT TESTAMENT

THE CONTINUANCE OF MY OLD AND NEW TESTAMENT, SAYS THE LORD GOD

"VOLUME THIRTY-THREE"

"IT IS A COMPLETION, SAYS THE LORD GOD AND THE BELIEVING VICTORIOUS ONES"

BY:

BARBARA ANN MARY MACK

BEGAN: MARCH 5, 2019

COMPLETED: MARCH 25, 2019

CONTENTS

DEDICATION 12
ACKNOWLEDGMENT 13
1. THE BLESSED LAMB 14
2. CHRIST *JESUS*, THE SACRIFICIAL LAMB OF GOD 24
3. IT IS A COMPLETION 55
4. MY SHEEP AND ME, *SAYS THE LORD JESUS* 66
5. ENTER MY LIVING BLOOD, *SAYS CHRIST JESUS* 77
6. SAVED BY THE POWER OF MY HOLY BLOOD, *SAYS CHRIST JESUS* 86
7. AND ALL WILL WITNESS THE POWER OF THE SACRIFICIAL LAMB OF GOD'S LIFE SAVING BLOOD, *SAYS CHRIST JESUS, THE SACRIFICED ONE* 101
8. BARBARA AND THE SACRED LIVING BLOOD OF *CHRIST JESUS*. 108
9. MARY, THE BLESSED MOTHER OF *CHRIST JESUS*, THE SACRIFICIAL LAMB OF GOD ALMIGHTY 141
10. PRAISE AND THE SACRIFICIAL BLOOD OF *CHRIST JESUS*, THE LAMB OF GOD 148

DEDICATION

TO: *CHRIST JESUS,* THE VICTORIOUS LAMB OF GOD

ACKNOWLEDGMENT

HALLELUJAH! HALLELUJAH, **TO CHRIST** *JESUS,* THE VICTORIOUS SACRIFICIAL LAMB OF GOD.

THE BLESSED LAMB

CHRIST JESUS: THE PRECIOUS LAMB

CHRIST JESUS, THE PRECIOUS LAMB, SPEAKING

I AM HE-
YES, THE PRECIOUS SACRIFICIAL LAMB OF *GOD, THE FATHER, THE ETERNAL ALMIGHTY.*
FOR *HOLY IS THE LAMB (CHRIST JESUS)*-
WHO CAME FORTH FROM THE ESSENCE OF *ALMIGHTY GOD, THE GREAT AND HOLY I AM (JEHOVAH).*
I AM *CHRIST JESUS*, THE PRECIOUS LAMB OF *OUR HEAVENLY GOD AND FATHER (JEHOVAH).*
I AM THE LAMB WHO MAKES IT POSSIBLE FOR MY LOVED ONES IN HEAVEN AND ON EARTH *COME TOGETHER.*
FOR *HOLY AM I*-
YES, THE LAMB OF GOD, WHO DESCENDED TO YOU FROM *HEAVEN'S SWEET SKY.*
FOR *HOLY AND REAL*-
IS THE BLOOD OF THE LAMB THAT SATAN AND HIS FOLLOWERS OF EVIL AND DESTRUCTION, *CANNOT TAKE NOR STEAL.*
FOR *HOLY AND TRUE*-
IS THE PRECIOUS LOVE OF THE LAMB OF GOD, THE FATHER, THAT WAS SENT FROM HEAVEN ABOVE TO *WORTHY YOU.*
MARCH 23, 2019

THE PRECIOUS BLOOD

CHRIST JESUS, THE PRECIOUS LAMB, SPEAKING

BEHOLD *MY PRECIOUS BLOOD*-
BEHOLD THE *GIFT OF MY HOLY LOVE!*
FOR *HOLY AND TRUE*-
IS THE PRECIOUS LIFE SAVING BLOOD THAT I, YOUR HOLY LORD AND GOD, *SEND TO BLESSED YOU.*

HOLY AND TRUE-
IS MY PRECIOUS AND PRICELESS BLOOD THAT WAS SHED ON SWEET CALVARY FOR *ALL OF YOU.*
FOR *HOLY, YOU SEE-*
IS THE PRECIOUS BLOOD THAT *CAME FROM BLESSED ME.*
LOOK, O BLESSED ONES!
ENTER MY LIFE SAVING BLOOD OF LIFE, O WORTHY *DAUGHTERS AND SONS!*
FOR *HOLY, YOU SEE-*
IS THE INVALUABLE BLOOD THAT WAS *SHED FOR THEE.*
COME UNTO ME, *O BELOVED ONES!*
COME INTO THE ARMS AND REALM OF HE *(CHRIST JESUS)* WHO HAS SACRIFICED HIS PRECIOUS BLOOD FOR *HIS WELL-LOVED LITTLE DAUGHTERS AND SONS!*
MARCH 23, 2019

THE BLOOD OF CHRIST JESUS INVITES THE POOR AND LONELY: IT INVITES THE RICH AND THE FAMOUS

CHRIST JESUS, THE PRECIOUS LAMB, SPEAKING

MY HOLY BLOOD INVITES THE *POOR AND THE LONELY.*
COME, DEAR ONES, AND SEEK THE HOLY WAY OF *CHRIST ALMIGHTY.*
FOR *HOLY, ETERNAL AND TRUE-*
IS THE VOICE AND SACRED BLOOD OF *HE* (CHRIST ALMIGHTY) *WHO CALLS YOU.*
MY BLOOD OF LOVE AND MERCY *INVITES THE RICH ONES TOO.*
COME, DEAR ONES, AND DO THE WORKS THAT *MY HEAVENLY FATHER AND I DO.*
HOLY IS *GOD, THE FATHER, ABOVE-*
FOR HE TOO, SENDS OUT *HIS INVITATION OF DIVINE MERCY AND LOVE.*
HOLY AND TRUE-
IS OUR HEAVENLY GOD AND FATHER, FOR *HE LOVES YOU TOO.*
HOLY IS HE-

YES, GOD, OUR FATHER, WHO HAS SENT TO YOU ALL, *BLESSED AND SACRIFICIAL LIFE SAVING HOLY ME.*
MARCH 23, 2019

THE PRECIOUS BLOOD AND *THE RICH AND FAMOUS*

CHRIST JESUS, THE PRECIOUS LAMB, SPEAKING

MY PRECIOUS BLOOD SENDS OUT INVITATIONS OF LOVE TO *THE RICH AND THE FAMOUS-*
SO THAT THEY TOO, WILL GAIN THE OPPORTUNITY TO FOLLOW THE LOVE AND *TEACHINGS OF SACRIFICIAL CHRIST JESUS.*
FOR *HOLY AND TRUE-*
IS THE BLOOD THAT WAS SHED FOR THE *RICH, AND THE FAMOUS ONES TOO.*
HOLY AND TRUE-
IS THE FAITHFUL BLOOD THAT CALLS THE RICH AND FAMOUS ONES TO *LIVE HOLY LIVES TOO.*
HOLY IS THE INVITING BLOOD OF *SACRIFICIAL CHRIST JESUS-*
ETERNAL IS THE LAMB OF GOD WHO *SEEKS THE RICH AND THE FAMOUS.*
HOLY AND TRUE-
IS THE BLOOD OF THE LAMB THAT *INVITES ALL OF YOU.*
MARCH 23, 2019

HOLY AND TRUE IS *THE PRICELESS BLOOD OF THE LAMB* THAT CONSTANTLY SEEKS AND CALLS BLESSED YOU

CHRIST JESUS, THE PRECIOUS LAMB, SPEAKING

MY DEAR CHILDREN-
MY LOVED ONES FROM *EVERY BLESSED NATION-*

BARBARA ANN MARY MACK

HOLY AND TRUE-
IS MY LIFE SAVING BLOOD THAT *CONSTANTLY SEEKS AND CALLS BLESSED YOU.*
FOR THE CALL OF *MY HOLY BLOOD-*
IS SENT OUT EVERY DAY TO THOSE WHOM *I TREASURE AND LOVE.*
MY HOLY BLOOD IS *SENT TO THE LOST ONES.*
IT IS SENT TO MY CALLED AND *LOVED DAUGHTERS AND SONS.*
FOR *HOLY AND TRUE-*
IS THE CALL THAT IS *SENT TO YOU.*
MY HOLY CALL IS *SENT OUT EVERY DAY-*
TO PREVENT MY WANDERING SHEEP FROM *FOLLOWING SATAN'S UNRIGHTEOUS AND UNHOLY WAY.*
FOR *HOLY AND TRUE-*
IS THE LIFE SAVING CALL THAT IS *SENT OUT TO SINKING YOU.*
HOLY IS THE *INVITATION AND CALL-*
THAT REFUSE TO LET *THE CHOSEN ONES FALL.*
MARCH 23, 2019

I WILL FOLLOW HIM: I WILL FOLLOW CHRIST JESUS, THE BLESSED AND BELOVED LAMB OF GOD

BARBARA SPEAKING TO CHRIST JESUS, THE BLESSED AND BELOVED LAMB OF GOD

LEAD ME-
LEAD YOUR SENT MESSENGER AND BRIDE (BARBARA), O SACRIFICIAL CHRIST ALMIGHTY.
LEAD ME THROUGH YOUR OPEN GATES,
FOR MY OBEDIENT SOUL WAITS.
I AM WAITING FOR THE LAMB OF GOD-
TO LEAD ME TO HIS CHOSEN FLOCK OF LOVE.
FOR HOLY AND TRUE-
IS THE LOVE THAT COMES WITH BLESSED YOU.
LEAD ME, O GREAT AND HOLY ONE-
LEAD ME, O SACRIFICIAL LAMB AND ONLY BEGOTTEN SON.
FOR HOLY AND REAL-
IS THE LOVE FOR YOU THAT I FEEL.
LEAD ME THROUGH YOUR OPEN DOOR,
SO THAT I WILL NOT HAVE TO SEARCH ANY MORE.
FOR HOLY AND TRUE-
IS THE PEACE THAT COMES WITH KNOWING AND FOLLOWING SACRED LIFE SAVING YOU.
LEAD ME, MY LORD GOD.
LEAD ME THROUGH YOUR OPEN GATES OF LOVE, SO THAT I MAY BOW IN THE PRESENCE OF YOUR HOLY PRECIOUS BLOOD. MARCH 25, 2019

BARBARA ANN MARY MACK

THE PURITY OF THE *NEW BORN UNBLEMISHED LAMB*

CHRIST JESUS, THE SACRIFICIAL LAMB OF GOD, SPEAKING

HOLY IS HE (THE NEW BORN LAMB)-
WHO WAS CREATED AND *FORMED BY BLESSED ME.*
HOLY IS *THE LAMB OF GOD* (CHRIST JESUS)-
HOLY IS HE (THE NEW BORN LAMB) WHO CAME FROM *THE REALM OF CHRIST JESUS' LOVE.*
FOR HE (THE NEW BORN LAMB)-
REPRESENTS *HOLY SACRIFICIAL ME.*
YES, *THE PURITY*-
OF THE LITTLE LAMB, IS BLESSED BY *HOLY ME.*
FOR I HAVE *CHOSEN, YOU SEE*-
THIS LITTLE LAMB- YES, *MY HEAVEN FORMED BABY.*
HOLY AND TRUE-
IS THIS LITTLE LAMB THAT I HAVE *GIVEN TO BLESSED YOU.*
YES, THIS LAMB *HAS BEEN CHOSEN*-
BY HE (CHRIST JESUS) WHO *RESIDES IN SWEET HEAVEN.*
FOR HOLY IS *MY GIFT OF LOVE* (THE LITTLE LAMB)-
THAT DESCENDED WITH ME FROM *SWEET HEAVEN ABOVE.*
HOLY, YOU SEE-
IS THE LITTLE LAMB THAT DESCENDED FROM THE GATES OF HEAVEN WITH *BLESSED ETERNAL ME.*
MARCH 25, 2019

I WILL FEED YOU IN THE PRESENCE OF THE WORLD, MY LAMBS

CHRIST JESUS, THE RISEN LAMB OF GOD, SPEAKING

I WILL FEED YOU-
I WILL GIVE DIVINE NOURISHMENT TO MY LITTLE LAMBS, AS YOU FOLLOW AND BELIEVE IN HE *(CHRIST JESUS)* WHO IS *ETERNAL AND TRUE.*
I WILL FEED YOU IN THE *PRESENCE OF THE WORLD.*
I WILL FEED MY HUNGRY *LITTLE BOY AND GIRL.*
FOR *HOLY AND TRUE-*
IS THE SACRIFICIAL LAMB WHO *FEEDS WORTHY YOU.*
HOLY, YOU SEE-
IS THE HEAVEN SENT FOOD THAT COMES WITH *KNOWING AND BELIEVING IN HOLY ME.*
FOR *I, THE SACRIFICED ONE-*
BRINGS FOOD TO *MY STARVING AND NEEDY DAUGHTER AND SON.*
MARCH 25, 2019

CHRIST JESUS, THE SACRIFICIAL LAMB OF GOD

WORTHY IS THE LAMB: *THE SLAUGHTERED CHRIST JESUS*

BARBARA SPEAKING

WORTHY IS HE (CHRIST *JESUS*)-
WORTHY IS THE LAMB WHO WAS **SLAUGHTERED ON SWEET CALVARY.**
WORTHY IS HE (CHRIST *JESUS*)-
WORTHY IS *CHRIST JESUS,* **THE SLAUGHTERED GOD ALMIGHTY.**
WORTHY IS CHRIST *JESUS*-
WORTHY IS THE FATHER'S LAMB WHO WAS SENT TO **DIE FOR BLESSED US.**
WORTHY AND **HOLY IS THE NAME** (CHRIST *JESUS*)-
OF HE WHO REVEALS EVERLASTING SPIRITUAL **LOVE AND FAME.**
WORTHY IS THE **SLAUGHTERED CHRIST** *JESUS*-
HOLY IS THE SACRIFICIAL LAMB (CHRIST *JESUS*) WHO DIED, SO THAT HE MAY **SAVE BLESSED US.**
WORTHY! WORTHY! WORTHY!
WORTHY IS THE **SLAUGHTERED CHRIST ALMIGHTY!**
MARCH 5, 2019

JESUS, JESUS, JESUS: THE HOLY SACRIFICIAL LAMB WHO SAVES BLESSED US

BARBARA SPEAKING

JESUS, JESUS, JESUS-
YOU ARE THE BLESSED AND HOLY SACRIFICIAL LAMB WHO **SAVES REPENTANT US.**
JESUS, O SWEET **LIFE SAVING,** *JESUS-*
YOU ARE THE HOLY LAMB AND VICTORIOUS KING WHO **SAVES BLESSED AND WORTHY US.**
JESUS, JESUS, O SWEET SACRIFICIAL **LAMB OF ALMIGHTY GOD-**
I PRAISE YOU, O HOLY ONE, FOR EXHIBITING **YOUR REALM OF DIVINE LOVE.**
OH SACRIFICIAL ONE-
OH GOD, THE FATHER'S, **ONLY BEGOTTEN SON.**
I THANK HOLY YOU FOR **YOUR SACRIFICIAL ACT OF LOVE.**
I THANK YOU FOR DESCENDING TO US FROM **SWEET HEAVEN ABOVE.**

Holy and *Righteous are you;*
Holy, eternal and true.
March 5, 2019

I walk in the Holy Presence and midst of the precious blood of *Christ, the sacrificial Lamb of God, as I greet those who do not believe*

Barbara Speaking

My body, spirit and soul walk in the midst of the *non-believing ones,* as I shared God's Holy love and presence with the *unbelieving daughters and sons.*
For, the precious life saving *Blood of Christ Jesus-*
Was shed, so that we may gain access to salvation that is *offered to all of us.*
For *Holy and True-*
Is the precious blood that was shed for *non-believing you.*
My blessed Spirit-
Speaks God's Holy life saving word to *all who will hear it.*
For *Holy is He (Christ Jesus)-*
Who has sent to the non-believing ones, *blessed me.*
March 12, 2019

I have shared your divine truth with *the unbelieving ones, Lord Jesus*

Barbara Speaking to the Lord *Jesus*

I, your sent messenger of *Divine Truth and Love,*
Have shared your good news that descended to me from *sweet heaven above.*
I have shared *your life saving truth-*
That was given to me *since my youth.*
I have spoken to the *non-believing one-*
About the Holy position of God, the Father's, *only begotten and sacrificial Son (Christ Jesus)-*
But they did not *heed or obey-*

THE GOOD NEWS THAT ALMIGHTY GOD *ASKED ME TO SAY*.

BARBARA SPEAKING TO THE NON-BELIEVERS

FOR *HOLY AND TRUE-*
IS THE BLOOD THAT WAS SHED FOR ME AND *NON-BELIEVING YOU.*
MARCH 12, 2019

THE LIFE-LESS BLOOD OF ANIMALS CANNOT SAVE YOU, *SAYS CHRIST JESUS, THE SACRIFICIAL LAMB OF GOD*

CHRIST JESUS, THE SACRIFICIAL LAMB OF GOD, SPEAKING

MY CHILDREN-
WILL YOU LISTEN?
FOR THE LIFE-LESS BLOOD OF YOUR SLAUGHTERED ANIMALS *CANNOT SAVE YOUR SINFUL SOULS TODAY.*
FOR I, THE LAMB OF GOD, HAVE COME TO SHOW AND LEAD YOU TO *MY LIFE SAVING HOLY WAY.*
FOR *THE LIFE-LESS BLOOD-*
THAT DOESN'T FLOW *FROM MY REALM ABOVE.*
THE LIFE-LESS BLOOD-
CANNOT SAVE AND FREE THOSE WHOM THE *FATHER AND I LOVE.*
MY CHILDREN: FLEE FROM *THE LIFE-LESS BLOOD-*
FOR IT CANNOT RELEASE THE *POWER OF MY LOVE.*
FOR, *HOLY IS THE BLOOD-*
THAT COMES FROM THE BODY OF HE *(CHRIST JESUS)* WHO LOVES AND REIGNS IN *SWEET HEAVEN ABOVE.*
MARCH 15, 2019

THE EVER-FLOWING BLOOD OF *CHRIST JESUS, THE SACRIFICIAL LAMB OF GOD,* THE FATHER

BARBARA SPEAKING OF THE BLOOD OF CHRIST JESUS, THE SACRIFICIAL LAMB OF ALMIGHTY GOD, THE FATHER

THE EVER-FLOWING **BLOOD OF CHRIST JESUS**-
HAS SANCTIFIED THOSE WHO **BELIEVE IN US** (THE BLESSED AND HOLY TRINITY AND BARBARA HIS CHOSEN BRIDE).
HOLY IS **THE EVER-FLOWING BLOOD**-
THAT SPEAKS TO ALL WHO HONOR AND RESPECT **HIS** (THE BLESSED AND HOLY TRINITY) **REALM OF DIVINE LOVE.**
FLOW, O PRECIOUS **BLOOD OF CHRIST JESUS**-
FLOW OVER THE BELIEVING ONES AS YOU **SHINE UPON BLESSED US.**
FOR **HOLY AND TRUE**-
ARE PRICELESS AND **EVER-FLOWING YOU.**
FLOW IN THE MIDST OF **YOUR FAITHFUL ONES**-
FLOW, O PRECIOUS BLOOD, OVER YOUR BLESSED AND **OBEDIENT DAUGHTERS AND SONS.**
LET THE HOLY HEAVENLY GATES THAT **RELEASED YOU**-
PERMIT THE BELIEVING ONES TO **ENTER THROUGH.**
FLOW, FLOW, FLOW, O PRECIOUS **LIFE SAVING BLOOD.**
FLOW OVER THOSE WHOM YOU HAVE SAVED BY THE POWER OF **YOUR INFINITE HOLY LOVE.**
MARCH 17, 2019

THE BLOOD: THE DIVINE LIGHT: THE SACRIFICIAL LAMB OF GOD: CHRIST JESUS

BARBARA SPEAKING

THE POWERFUL **BLOOD OF CHRIST JESUS**-
SENDS THE GREAT AND HOLY LIGHT THAT **LEADS BLESSED US.**
THE BLOOD AND **HOLY LIGHT**-
ARE RELEASED BY THE SACRIFICIAL LAMB THROUGH **HIS GREAT MIGHT.**
HOLY IS **THE LAMB'S BLOOD AND LIGHT**-
THAT PIERCE THE **WORLD'S DARKEST SIN AND NIGHT.**
FOR, HOLY, HOLY, **HOLY, YOU SEE**-
ARE THE BLOOD AND LIGHT THAT THE SACRIFICIAL LAMB **GIVES TO BLESSED YOU AND ME.**

HOLY IS CHRIST JESUS-
SACRED IS THE BLOOD THAT WAS **SHED FOR US.**
MARCH 17, 2019

OH, HOW SWEET IT IS: *THE PRECIOUS AND PRICELESS BLOOD OF LIFE*

<u>**BARBARA SPEAKING OF THE BLOOD OF CHRIST JESUS, THE SACRIFICIAL LAMB OF ALMIGHTY GOD, THE FATHER**</u>

HOW SWEET IT IS-
YES, THE HOLY LIFE SAVING BLOOD **THAT IS HIS** (CHRIST JESUS).
FOR **HOLY AND TRUE-**
IS THE PRECIOUS BLOOD THAT **SAVES BLESSED ME AND YOU.**
HOW SWEET THE TASTE OF **CHRIST JESUS' HOLY BLOOD-**
THAT DESCENDED WITH HIM FROM **SWEET HEAVEN ABOVE.**
HOLY IS THE TASTE OF THE BLOOD OF **CHRIST JESUS, THE SLAUGHTERED ONE.**
HOLY IS GOD, THE FATHER'S, **ONLY BEGOTTEN SACRIFICIAL SON.**
MARCH 17, 2019

THE SACRIFICIAL BLOOD: *THE HOLY JUDGE*

<u>**ALMIGHTY GOD, THE FATHER, SPEAKING**</u>

HOLY AND TRUE-
IS THE BLOOD THAT **JUDGES YOU.**
HOLY AND ETERNAL IS HE (CHRIST JESUS)-
WHO HAS SHED **HIS PRECIOUS BLOOD FOR THEE.**
FOR **THE SACRIFICIAL BLOOD-**
JUDGES THOSE WHOM **GOD, THE FATHER, DO LOVE.**
FOR HOLY IS HE (CHRIST JESUS)-
WHO HAS SACRIFICED HIS PRECIOUS LIFE AND **BLOOD FOR THEE.**
FOR THE BLOOD OF **THE HOLY JUDGE HAS SPOKEN-**
TO EVERYTHING AND **EVERY NATION.**
FOR HOLY IS **THE BLOOD, YOU SEE-**
THAT JUDGES THE CHILDREN OF **GOD ALMIGHTY.**
FAITHFUL AND TRUE-

IS THE BLOOD THAT *JUDGES REPENTANT YOU.*
FAITHFUL AND EVERLASTING-
IS THE BLOOD OF *CHRIST*, THE SACRIFICIAL LAMB AND *TRIUMPHANT KING.*
MARCH 18, 2019

MY LOST SHEEP HEAR AND FOLLOW THE HOLY CALL AND PRESENCE OF MY LIVING LIFE SAVING BLOOD, SAYS CHRIST JESUS, THE SLAUGHTERED SACRIFICIAL LAMB OF GOD, THE FATHER

CHRIST *JESUS,* THE SLAUGHTERED SACRIFICIAL LAMB OF GOD, THE FATHER, SPEAKING

THEY HAVE HEARD AND FOLLOWED THE HOLY CALL OF *MY PRECIOUS BLOOD;*
AND NOW, THEIR BLESSED SOULS LIVE WITHIN THE *REALM OF MY LOVE.*
FOR *HOLY IS HE-*
WHO HEARS AND FOLLOWS THE *SACRED BLOOD OF CHRIST ALMIGHTY.*
HOLY IS HE-
WHO HEARS AND FOLLOWS THE SACRED BLOOD THAT CAME FROM *SACRIFICIAL ME.*
FOR *MY LOST LITTLE ONES-*
HAVE BECOME *MY BELIEVING DAUGHTERS AND SONS.*
FOR *RIGHTEOUS ARE THEY-*
WHO FOLLOW MY BLOOD, AND *MY HOLY LIFE SAVING WAY.*
HOLY AND TRUE-
IS THE PRECIOUS BLOOD THAT *CALLS WORTHY YOU.*
MARCH 18, 2019

THE PRECIOUS BLOOD OF THE MERCIFUL LAMB OF GOD LED ME TO NON-BELIEVING THEE

BARBARA SPEAKING TO THOSE WHO DO NOT BELIEVE IN THE DIVINE POWER OF THE BLOOD OF CHRIST *JESUS,* THE SACRIFICIAL LAMB OF GOD, THE FATHER

THE HOLY BLOOD OF *CHRIST ALMIGHTY-*
LED ME TO THOSE WHOM HE HAS OFFERED *HIS LOVE AND MERCY.*
AS THE NON-BELIEVERS *REJECT ME-*

THEY ALSO REJECT THE HOLY LIFE SAVING BLOOD OF *CHRIST ALMIGHTY.*
FOR HOLY IS THE *LAMB'S BLOOD, YOU SEE-*
FOR IT HAS SENT *CHOSEN AND OBEDIENT ME.*
HOLY IS THE BLOOD-
THAT REVEALS GOD, THE FATHER'S, *REALM OF TRUE LOVE.*
HOLY AND TRUE-
IS THE BLOOD OF *CHRIST JESUS,* THAT WAS SENT TO *NON-BELIEVING YOU.*
MARCH 18, 2019

BARBARA: A CHOSEN VESSEL THAT HOLDS AND HOUSES THE PRECIOUS BLOOD OF CHRIST JESUS, THE SACRIFICIAL LAMB OF THE LIVING GOD

BARBARA SPEAKING

A VESSEL, **CHOSEN BY HE** (CHRIST JESUS)-
TO CARRY THE SACRED SPIRITUAL **BLOOD OF CHRIST ALMIGHTY**.
FOR, **CHOSEN AM I**-
TO CARRY THE PRECIOUS BLOOD THAT THE BELIEVING ONES WILL **NEVER DENY**.
FOR **HOLY IS HE** (CHRIST JESUS)-
WHO SACRIFICED HIS PRECIOUS LIFE AND BLOOD FOR **CHOSEN AND SENT ME**.
FOR, I CARRY THE SACRED BLOOD OF HE (CHRIST JESUS) WHOM **I TREASURE, ADORE, AND LOVE**.
FOR **HOLY IS HE** (CHRIST JESUS)-
WHO SHED HIS PRECIOUS BLOOD **FOR ME**.
HOLY AND WORTHY-
IS THE PRECIOUS BLOOD OF LIFE SAVING **CHRIST, THE ALMIGHTY**.
FOR, I HAVE BEEN **CHOSEN, YOU SEE**-
TO CARRY THE PRECIOUS LIFE SAVING BLOOD THAT WAS SHED FOR US, BY THE LIVING GOD AND KING, **CHRIST JESUS, THE ALMIGHTY**.
HOLY, HOLY, HOLY-
IS THE CHOSEN BRIDE (BARBARA) THAT HOLDS WITHIN HER, THE SACRIFICIAL BLOOD THAT FLOWED FROM THE BLESSED WOUNDS OF **GOD ALMIGHTY**.
HOLY, HOLY, HOLY-
ARE THE WOUNDS THAT RELEASED THE PRECIOUS BLOOD OF **HOLY INFINITE HE** (CHRIST JESUS).
MARCH 18, 2019

THE FREELY GIVEN BLOOD OF *THE SACRIFICIAL LAMB*

CHRIST JESUS, THE SACRIFICIAL LAMB OF GOD, SPEAKING

MY CHILDREN-
YES, EVERYONE OF **MY GREAT CREATION**.
COME AND SEE-
THE WONDERFUL SACRIFICED THAT **I HAVE MADE FOR BLESSED THEE**.
COME AND **WITNESS THE LOVE**-
THAT FLOWS FROM **MY LIFE SAVING BLOOD**.
FOR **HOLY AND TRUE**-

IS THE GIFT THAT *I HAVE GIVEN FREELY TO ALL OF YOU.*
MARCH 18, 2019

MY CHILDREN: REMEMBER THE BLOOD; REMEMBER THE FLOWING BLOOD THAT SAVED YOU, *SAYS CHRIST JESUS, THE SACRIFICIAL LAMB OF GOD*

CHRIST *JESUS,* THE SACRIFICIAL LAMB OF GOD, SPEAKING

MY CHILDREN:
O BLESSED ONES FROM *EVERY NATION.*
REMEMBER *MY BLOOD OF LIFE,*
AS IT SAVES YOUR BLESSED SOULS FROM THE DESTRUCTION AND PAIN OF *WORLDLY CONFUSION AND STRIFE.*
REMEMBER *ITS HOLY POWER-*
THAT SAVES THE BLESSED SOULS *EVERY SECOND, MINUTE AND HOUR.*
FOR *HOLY AND TRUE-*
IS THE POWERFUL BLOOD THAT *SANCTIFIES YOU.*
REMEMBER SACRIFICIAL ME-
REMEMBER, DEAR CHILDREN, THE POWERFUL BLOOD THAT *I HAVE SHED FOR BLESSED THEE.*
FOR *HOLY AND TRUE-*
IS THE PRECIOUS BLOOD THAT *REWARDS AND SAVES BLESSED YOU.*
MARCH 18, 2019

BARBARA ANN MARY MACK
THE TRIUMPHANT BLOOD OF THE LAMB HAS *RESCUED ME*

BARBARA SPEAKING

THE TRIUMPHANT BLOOD OF *CHRIST JESUS*, THE SACRIFICIAL LAMB OF GOD, HAS **RESCUED ME.**
FOR I FOLLOW THE HOLY VOICE AND CALL OF **CHRIST ALMIGHTY.**
THE TRIUMPHANT BLOOD HAS **RESCUED HIS LOVED ONES-**
IT HAS RESCUED AND SAVED THE LAMB'S WORTHY AND **VICTORIOUS DAUGHTERS AND SONS.**
THE TRIUMPHANT BLOOD HAS RESCUED **GOD'S FAITHFUL AND OBEDIENT LOVED ONES.**
THE SACRIFICIAL BLOOD HAS SAVED **THE LAMB'S OBEDIENT DAUGHTERS AND SONS.**
WORTHY AND TRUE-
IS THE TRIUMPHANT BLOOD THAT WAS **SHED FOR ME AND YOU.**
HOLY IS THE PRECIOUS BLOOD OF **CHRIST JESUS, THE SACRIFICED ONE.**
TRIUMPHANT IS THE LAMB OF **GOD, THE FATHER'S, VICTORIOUS SON.**
FOR, **HOLY AND TRUE-**
IS THE *CHRIST*, WHO **DIED FOR ME AND YOU.**
HOLY IS HE (*CHRIST JESUS*)-
WHO HAS SHED HIS PRECIOUS TRIUMPHANT BLOOD FOR **BLESSED AND BELOVED YOU AND ME.**
MARCH 18, 2019

THE EVERLASTING POWER OF THE SACRIFICIAL BLOOD OF THE LAMB HAS CAPTURED OUR BLESSED MINDS AND SOULS

BARBARA SPEAKING

THE POWER OF **THE HOLY BLOOD-**
HAS CAPTURED THE SOULS OF THOSE WHOM THE **SACRIFICIAL LAMB DOES LOVE.**
THE HOLY POWER-
PROTECTS THE BELIEVING ONES **EVERY DAY AND HOUR.**
FOR **HOLY IS THE BLOOD-**
THAT RELEASES **DIVINE LOVE.**
THROUGHOUT EACH DAY-

BARBARA ANN MARY MACK

THE HOLY POWER OF THE LAMB'S BLOOD LEADS HIS FLOCK TO *HIS SAFE AND SECURED HOLY WAY.*
FOR *HOLY, EVERLASTING AND TRUE-*
IS THE SACRED BLOOD OF HE *(CHRIST JESUS)* WHO HAS *BLESSED ME AND YOU.*
SACRED AND GRAND-
IS THE PRECIOUS FLOWING LIFE SAVING BLOOD THAT LEADS US TO *GOD'S PROMISE LAND.*
MARCH 18, 2019

ON THE ROAD THAT LEADS TO THE PRECIOUS BLOOD OF *CHRIST JESUS*, THE SACRIFICIAL LAMB OF GOD, THE FATHER

BARBARA SPEAKING

I AM ON THE ROAD THAT *LEADS TO THEE* (CHRIST *JESUS*)-
I AM ON THE ROAD THAT LEADS TO THE PRECIOUS AND PRICELESS BLOOD THAT WAS *SHED FOR ME.*
I AM ON THE *ROAD THAT LEADS*-
TO THE TRIUMPHANT BLOOD OF THE SACRIFICIAL LAMB WHO *ALWAYS FEEDS.*
HE FEEDS HIS FOLD-
WITH THE KNOWLEDGE OF *HEAVENLY GOLD* (WORDS OF TRUTH).
FOR HIS PRECIOUS *BLOOD OF LIFE*-
HAS NOURISHED AND FED ME, *HIS HEAVEN FORMED WIFE.*
HOLY AND TRUE IS HE (CHRIST *JESUS*)-
WHO LEADS AND *GUIDES OBEDIENT ME.*
FOR ON THE *ROAD TO ETERNAL LIFE*-
I AM REMOVED FROM *THIS WORLD'S SIN AND STRIFE.*
FOR *HOLY, YOU SEE*-
IS THE ROAD THAT *LEADS OBEDIENT ME.*
MARCH 19, 2019

CHRIST JESUS, THE HOLY SOUND OF *CONTINUOUS LOVE AND MERCY*

BARBARA SPEAKING

CHRIST *JESUS,* CHRIST *JESUS!*
HE IS THE HOLY SOUND THAT *SAVES BLESSED US!*
HOLY IS THE NAME-
THAT EXHIBITS *EVERLASTING SPIRITUAL FAME.*
FOR *HOLY AND TRUE*-
IS THE ETERNAL NAME THAT *CALLS BLESSED ME AND YOU.*
HOLY IS HE (CHRIST *JESUS*)-
WHO HAS SACRIFICED HIS PRECIOUS NAME AND BLOOD FOR *BLESSED AND CALLED YOU AND ME.*
THE SOUND-
YES, IS *ALWAYS AROUND.*
FOR HOLY IS THE NAME AND *BLOOD OF CHRIST JESUS*-
ETERNAL IS GOD, THE SON, WHO WAS SENT TO *WORTHY AND BELIEVING US.*

FOR *HOLY AND TRUE*-
IS THE NAME AND *GOD WHO DOES RESCUE*.
HE SAVES US-
BY THE LIVING POWER AND LOVE OF *SACRIFICIAL CHRIST JESUS*.
FOR *HOLY, ETERNAL AND TRUE*-
IS THE NAME THAT *SEES US THROUGH*.
HOLY, HOLY, HOLY-
IS THE PERFECT NAME OF *CHRIST ALMIGHTY!*
FOR *HOLY AND TRUE*-
IS THE NAME OF THE SACRIFICIAL LAMB OF GOD WHO *COMES TO ME AND YOU*.
MARCH 20, 2019

MY BLOOD OF LIGHT WILL NOT LEAVE YOU IN THE DARK, SAYS CHRIST JESUS, THE SACRIFICIAL LAMB OF ALMIGHTY GOD

CHRIST *JESUS*, THE SACRIFICIAL LAMB OF ALMIGHTY GOD, SPEAKING

COME WITH ME-
ALL WHO *DESIRE TO BE FREE*.
COME, AND TAKE *MY LIFE SAVING HAND,*
SO THAT I MAY LEAD YOU TO *MY PROMISED RADIANT LAND*.
COME AND EXPERIENCE-
THE DEPTH OF MY LOVE, AND *MY HOLY PRESENCE*.
THERE, *YOU WILL SEE*-
THE SACRED LIGHT AND BLOOD THAT *SAVES WORTHY THEE*.
DEAR CHILDREN: *COME WITH ME*-
TO THE LAND THAT IS ETERNAL, *LIFE GIVING AND FREE!*
MARCH 20, 2019

AND *CHRIST JESUS,* THE SACRIFICIAL LAMB OF GOD, BECAME FLESH, *AND* LIVED IN THE MIDST OF BLESSED US

BARBARA SPEAKING

AND THE SACRIFICIAL *LAMB OF GOD*-
BECAME FLESH, AND LIVED IN THE MIDST OF THOSE WHOM *HE CREATED OUT OF DIVINE LOVE.*
FOR *HOLY AND REAL*-
WAS THE SACRIFICIAL LAMB WHOM HIS CALLED AND CHOSEN FOLLOWERS COULD *SEE AND FEEL.*
YES, HE, ALMIGHTY GOD, THE SON, *LIVED IN THE MIDST OF US*-
IN THE FORM OF HOLY AND *BLESSED CHRIST JESUS.*
FOR *HOLY AND REAL*-
WAS THE SACRIFICIAL LAMB WHO *ALL COULD SEE AND FEEL.*
HOLY AND TRUE-
IS THE SACRIFICIAL GOD *(CHRIST JESUS)* WHO BECAME LIVING FLESH, SO THAT HE MAY *LIVE ON EARTH WITH BLESSED YOU.*
MARCH 21, 2019

I AM NOT OF THIS WORLD, *SAYS CHRIST JESUS, THE SACRIFICIAL LAMB OF GOD*

CHRIST *JESUS,* THE SACRIFICIAL LAMB OF GOD, SPEAKING

I AM NOT OF *THIS PASSING CORRUPTED WORLD*-
LISTEN TO ME, O BLESSED *LITTLE BOY AND GIRL.*
LISTEN TO *MY HOLY WORDS OF LOVE*-
THAT DESCENDED WITH ME FROM *SWEET HEAVEN ABOVE.*
FOR *HOLY AND TRUE*-
IS THE SACRIFICIAL LAMB WHO *DESCENDED TO YOU.*
I AM NOT OF THIS PASSING WORLD, O BLESSED *CHILDREN OF MINE,*
FOR I EXISTED BEFORE THE REALM OF *HUMAN CREATED TIME.*
FOR *HOLY AND TRUE*-
IS THE SON OF GOD, WHO *DESCENDED TO YOU.*
MARCH 21, 2019

CHRIST JESUS' MANY WOUNDS HAVE RELEASED THE ENTRANCE TO EVERLASTING LIFE

BARBARA SPEAKING TO THE WOUNDS OF CHRIST *JESUS*, THE SACRIFICIAL LAMB OF GOD

YOU HAVE RELEASED THE ENTRANCE TO *SWEET HEAVEN ABOVE*,
BY THE POWER AND MIGHTY WORKS OF *YOUR HOLY LOVE*.
O PRECIOUS WOUNDS OF *CHRIST ALMIGHTY*-
I PRAISE AND BLESS YOU FOR *LEADING OBEDIENT ME*.
FOR YOU HAVE *LED ME*-
IN THE DIRECTION OF THE *SACRIFICIAL CHRIST ALMIGHTY*.
AND NOW *I CAN SEE*-
THE HOLY ENTRANCE THAT *BECKONS ME*.
FOR *HOLY, HOLY, HOLY*-
ARE THE WOUNDS AND PRECIOUS BLOOD OF *GOD ALMIGHTY*!
MARCH 10, 2019

IT, THE PRECIOUS BLOOD OF THE SACRIFICIAL LAMB OF GOD, HAS *PURIFIED THE SOULS OF THE RIGHTEOUS AND HOLY ONES*

BARBARA SPEAKING

IT-
YES, THE PRECIOUS BLOOD THAT REVEALS *THE SLAUGHTERED LAMB'S BLESSED HOLY SPIRIT*-
HAS PURIFIED ME-
IT HAS PURIFIED THE SOUL OF *THE RIGHTEOUS AND THE HOLY*.
THE BLOOD THAT HAS *CLEANSED ME*-
WAS SHED ON *SWEET CALVARY*.
FOR *HOLY AND TRUE*-
IS THE SACRIFICIAL ONE *(CHRIST JESUS)* WHO WAS *SLAIN FOR ME AND YOU*.
HOLY IS *THE LAMB OF GOD*-
WHO HAS PURIFIED THOSE *WHO ARE LOVED*.
HOLY AND RIGHTEOUS-
ARE THEY WHO FOLLOW *GOD'S UNENDING REALM OF GOODNESS*.
FOR *HOLY IS HE*-
WHO RECEIVES THE GIFT OF THE SACRIFICIAL *LAMB'S LOVE AND MERCY*.
FOR *HOLY AND TRUE*-

BARBARA ANN MARY MACK

IS THE PRICELESS BLOOD THAT HAS WASHED AND CLEANSED *BLESSED ME AND YOU.*
HOLY AND TRUE ARE *THE RIGHTEOUS ONES-*
SAVED AND BLESSED ARE THE *LAMB'S DAUGHTERS AND SONS.*
MARCH 19, 2019

COMPASSIONATE LIKE *CHRIST JESUS*, THE SACRIFICIAL ONE

CHRIST JESUS, THE SACRIFICIAL ONE, SPEAKING

I WANT ALL TO BE-
COMPASSIONATE AND MERCIFUL LIKE HOLY ME.
I WANT MY DAUGHTERS AND SONS-
TO BE LOVING AND KIND TO THE NEEDY ONES.
FOR HOLY, YOU SEE-
IS THE FLOWING BLOOD OF COMPASSIONATE CHRIST ALMIGHTY.
I WANT MY CHOSEN ONES TO KNOW-
THAT I DESIRE THAT THEY SHOW MERCY AND COMPASSION WHEREVER THEY GO.
FOR HOLY, HOLY, HOLY-
IS LOVING, MERCIFUL, AND COMPASSIONATE CHRIST ALMIGHTY.
MY DEAR CHILDREN, EXHIBIT ME-
EXHIBIT THE DIVINE LOVE OF GOD ALMIGHTY.
FOR HOLY, YOU SEE-
IS THE BLOOD THAT FLOWED FROM COMPASSIONATE SACRIFICIAL ME.
MARCH 21, 2019

LORD JESUS: UPON YOUR BLESSED SHOULDERS WERE PLACED THE SINS OF THE WORLD

ALMIGHTY GOD, THE FATHER, SPEAKING TO CHRIST JESUS, HIS ONLY BEGOTTEN SON

MY SON:
IT WAS UPON YOUR BLESSED SACRIFICIAL SHOULDERS THAT THE SINS OF THE WORLD WERE TAKEN ON BY CHRIST JESUS, THE HOLY ONE.
UPON YOUR SHOULDERS OF LOVE-
THE SINS OF THE WORLD WERE PLACED UPON HE (CHRIST JESUS) WHO DESCENDED FROM SWEET HEAVEN ABOVE.
FOR HOLY, YOU SEE-
IS CHRIST, THE ALMIGHTY.

BARBARA SPEAKING TO THE SACRIFICIAL LORD JESUS

HOLY AND TRUE-
IS HE *(CHRIST JESUS)* WHO DID BEAR THE SINS OF THE WORLD, AS HE CARRIED *THE FATHER'S DIVINE ASSIGNMENT THROUGH.*
FOR *YOUR SACRIFICIAL ACT OF LOVE-*
DESCENDED WITH YOU *FROM HEAVEN ABOVE.*
LORD *JESUS:* UPON *YOUR BLESSED SHOULDERS OF LOVE-*
WAS THE HEAVENLY STRENGTH THAT *DESCENDED FROM ABOVE.*
FOR *HOLY AND TRUE-*
IS HE *(CHRIST JESUS)* CARRIED THE FATHER'S ASSIGNMENT OF *LOVE THROUGH.*
HOLY IS HE (CHRIST JESUS)-
WHO BORE THE SINS OF THE WORLD, *AND ME.*
HOLY IS HE (CHRIST JESUS)-
WHO HAS WASHED AWAY THE SINS THAT *TORMENTED ME. MARCH 22, 2019*

BARBARA: A MESSENGER OF CHRIST JESUS, THE TRUE LIVING SACRIFICIAL LIGHT OF THE WORLD

BARBARA SPEAKING

HOLY AND *SENT BY HE* (CHRIST *JESUS*)-
WHO HAS *CHOSEN WORTHY ME.*
FOR *HIS POWERFUL LIGHT-*
HAS REVEALED THROUGH ME, *HIS HEAVEN SENT HOLY MIGHT.*
FOR *HOLY IS HE* (CHRIST *JESUS*)-
WHO LIVES THROUGH, AND WITHIN *PURIFIED ME.*
HOLY AND TRUE-
ARE THE MESSAGES THAT *HE SENDS TO BLESSED YOU.*
HOLY AND ETERNAL, *YOU SEE-*
IS THE SACRED BLOOD THAT SHINES *BEFORE, BEHIND, AND THROUGH BLESSED ME.*
FOR I AM THE *LAMB'S MESSENGER OF DIVINE LOVE-*
THAT WAS SENT FROM *SWEET HEAVEN ABOVE.*
MARCH 22, 2019

I WILL NEVER FORGET, MY LORD GOD. I WILL NEVER FORGET YOUR SACRIFICIAL ACT OF LOVE

BARBARA SPEAKING TO THE LORD GOD, THE SACRIFICIAL LAMB

I WILL NEVER FORGET, MY GOD.
I WILL NEVER FORGET *YOUR SACRIFICIAL ACT OF HOLY LOVE.*
FOR *HOLY AND TRUE-*
IS THE DIVINE ACT OF LOVE THAT WAS *PERFORMED BY YOU.*
FOR *HOLY AND TRUE-*
ARE THE WONDERFUL HOLY THINGS THAT *YOU SO LOVINGLY DO.*
I WILL NEVER, NEVER, NEVER FORGET, *O HOLY ONE* (CHRIST *JESUS*).
I WILL NEVER FORGET THE SACRIFICIAL ACT LOVE THAT WAS DONE FOR US BY ALMIGHTY GOD, THE FATHER'S, *ONLY BEGOTTEN SON* (CHRIST *JESUS*).
FOR *HOLY AND TRUE-*
ARE GRACIOUS AND *GLORIOUS YOU.*
I WILL NEVER FORGET *YOUR SACRIFICIAL ACT OF LOVE-*
YOUR ABUSE; YOUR SCOURGING; YOUR SUFFERING; AND YOUR DEATH ON THE CROSS, THAT DESCENDED TO US FROM *SWEET HEAVEN ABOVE.*

FOR, *I TRULY LOVE YOU.*
I TRULY LOVE *EVERY BLESSED THING THAT YOU DO.*
MY LORD *JESUS:* NO ONE NOR THING *WILL CAUSE ME-*
TO FORGET THE SACRIFICIAL ACT OF DIVINE LOVE THAT *YOU DID FOR ME.*
I WILL NEVER FORGET THE SACRIFICIAL ACT OF *CHRIST, THE ALMIGHTY.*
I WILL NEVER FORGET THE MAGNITUDE OF THE LOVE THAT *YOU EXPRESSED FOR BLESSED ME*
FOR *HOLY IS HE* (CHRIST *JESUS*)-
WHO WAS ABUSED AND SCOURGED FOR *LOWLY ME.*
MY LORD *JESUS: NO ONE NOR THING-*
COULD EVER CAUSE ME TO FORGET OR DENY THE HOLY CRUCIFIXION OF *CHRIST ALMIGHTY; MY EVERLASTING KING.*

BARBARA SPEAKING TO GOD'S CALLED AND CHOSEN ONES

FOR *HOLY IS HE* (CHRIST *JESUS*)-
WHO WAS *CRUCIFIED FOR ME.*
HOLY AND TRUE-
IS THE LAMB WHO WAS *SCOURGED FOR ME AND YOU.*
HOLY, HOLY, HOLY-
IS CHRIST ALMIGHTY!
I WILL NEVER FORGET, *YOU SEE-*
THE HOLY DEATH OF *CHRIST ALMIGHTY.*
MARCH 22, 2019

MY BLESSED AND LOVELY DAUGHTER (LA TOYA): LET YOU AND I DELIVER THE PRECIOUS LIFE SAVING BLOOD OF CHRIST JESUS

BARBARA SPEAKING TO LA TOYA, HER BLESSED DAUGHTER

O LOVELY *GOD SENT ONE* (LA TOYA)-
LET US DELIVER THE HOLY WORDS THAT LEAD TO THE SACRIFICIAL LAMB OF GOD'S SACRED BLOOD OF LIFE, THAT ARE OFFERED BY *GOD, THE FATHER'S, ONLY BEGOTTEN SON* (CHRIST *JESUS*).
LA TOYA: LET YOU AND I *DELIVER TODAY-*

THE HOLY WORDS OF JESUS' LIFE SAVING BLOOD THAT LEAD TO **HIS DIVINE TRUTH AND WAY.**

LA TOYA: LET **YOU AND I-**
DELIVER THE HOLY WORDS OF GOD, WHOSE DWELLING PLACE IS **ABOVE THE DIVINELY MADE SKY.**

LET YOU AND I SEEK-
THE LOST SOULS OF THE SPIRITUALLY BLINDED ONES **AND THE MEEK.**

FOR **HOLY AND TRUE-**
IS THE SACRED BLOOD OF CHRIST JESUS, WHO **SENT BLESSED ME AND YOU.**

FOR **HOLY YOU, SEE-**
IS THE PRECIOUS BLOOD OF THE LAMB, THAT GUIDES BLESSED AND **WELL-LOVED THEE.**

HOLY AND TRUE-
IS THE POWER OF THE PRICELESS BLOOD THAT HAS **SENT BLESSED AND OBEDIENT YOU.**

MARCH 23, 2019

AMYA: LET US LOVE AND CLING TO THE FULFILLED PROMISES OF THE BLOOD OF CHRIST JESUS, THE SACRIFICIAL LAMB OF ALMIGHTY GOD, THE FATHER

BARBARA SPEAKING TO AMYA, HER BLESSED AND WELL-LOVED GRANDDAUGHTER

AMYA; O CHOSEN AND **BLESSED DAUGHTER-**
OF OUR **HOLY GOD, THE FATHER.**

AMYA: LET US-
CONTINUE IN THE LOVE THAT WAS SHED WITH THE BLOOD OF OUR **SAVIOR AND GOD, CHRIST JESUS.**

AMYA: LET US HOLD ON TO THE PROMISES THAT WERE **FULFILLED, AND WILL LAST,**
AS WE GRACIOUSLY REMEMBER **HIS HOLY PRESENCE IN OUR PAST.**

FOR **HOLY AND REAL-**
ARE THE FULFILLED PROMISES THAT YOU CAN **FOREVER SEE AND FEEL.**

FOR **HOLY AND TRUE-**
IS THE GOD WHO MADE **MANY PROMISES TO ME AND YOU.**

HOLY AND REAL-

ARE THE PROMISES THAT WERE TO YOU AND ME, *MANIFESTED AND FULFILLED.*
FOR *HOLY AND TRUE-*
IS THE SACRIFICIAL LAMB OF GOD WHO *TRULY LOVES BLESSED YOU.*
FOR YOU CAN *TRULY SEE-*
THE HOLY PRESENCE AND POWER OF *CHRIST JESUS; GOD ALMIGHTY.*

MARCH 23, 2019

THE CALL: *THE SANCTIFIED CALL OF THE LIVING SACRIFICIAL LAMB OF ALMIGHTY GOD, THE FATHER*

THE LIVING SACRIFICIAL LAMB OF ALMIGHTY GOD, THE FATHER, SPEAKING

O BLESSED CHILDREN OF THE SACRIFICIAL *LAMB OF GOD, THE FATHER-*
COME TO ME, AS MY LOVED ONES, AROUND *ME, GATHER.*
COME TO *MY REALM OF DIVINE TRUTH-*
THAT SOME OF YOU DID NOT RECEIVE FROM ME, *IN YOUR YOUTH.*
FOR *HOLY, YOU SEE-*
IS THE LAMB THAT CALLS AND SUMMONS *BLESSED THEE.*
FOR *HOLY AND TRUE-*
IS THE CALL THAT *I SEND OUT TO YOU.*
HOLY IS THIS DAY-
FOR I NOW, DESIRE THAT YOU SEEK AND FOLLOW *MY LIFE SAVING HOLY WORD AND WAY.*
FOR *HOLY AND TRUE-*
IS THE GOD AND FATHER WHO *SUMMONS WORTHY YOU.*
HOLY YOU SEE-
IS THE VOICE AND LOVE THAT ARE *SENT TO THEE.*
HOLY AND TRUE-
IS THE HEAVENLY FATHER WHO *TRULY LOVES BLESSED YOU.*

MARCH 23, 2019

I CAME INTO THE WORLD IN THE FORM OF FLESH AND BLOOD, SO THAT I MAY SAVE THE SOULS OF THE LOST ONES, SAYS CHRIST JESUS, THE SACRIFICIAL LAMB OF GOD, THE FATHER

CHRIST *JESUS,* THE SACRIFICIAL LAMB OF GOD, THE FATHER, SPEAKING

MY CHILDREN-
YES, YOU FROM **EVERY NATION**.
I CAME INTO THIS WORLD-
TO SAVE AND REDEEM THE SOULS OF THE **SINFUL BOY AND GIRL**.
I CAME IN THE FORM OF **FLESH AND BLOOD**,
SO THAT I MAY SAVE YOU BY THE POWER AND PRESENCE OF **MY HOLY LOVE**.
FOR **HOLY IS HE** (CHRIST JESUS)-
WHO CAME TO **SAVE BLESSED THEE**.
I WALKED AMONG YOU, **NOT SO LONG AGO**;
AND NOW, I HAVE MANY THINGS TO SAY, SO THAT **YOU MAY KNOW**.
I HAVE COME AGAIN, YOU SEE-
IN THE BLESSED AND PURIFIED FORM OF **BARBARA**, WHO WAS SENT BY **THE FATHER AND ME**.
FOR **HOLY AND TRUE**-
IS THE LOVE THAT **WE** (GOD, THE FATHER, AND CHRIST JESUS, THE SACRIFICIAL AND ONLY BEGOTTEN SON) **HAVE FOR BLESSED YOU**.
I HAVE COME TO **REVEAL MY LOVE**-
IN THE FORM OF MY LIVING WORDS OF TRUTH AND **MY LIFE SAVING BLOOD**.
FOR **HOLY, YOU SEE**-
IS THE ONE (BARBARA) WHOM **I SEND TO THEE**.
HOLY IS SHE (BARBARA)-
WHO REPRESENTS THE BLOOD OF **CHRIST, THE SACRIFICIAL ALMIGHTY**.
MARCH 24, 2019

REST WITHIN ME, SAYS THE LORD JESUS

THE LORD JESUS SPEAKING

REST, DEAR ONES-
REST WITHIN MY LIFE SAVING BLOOD, O BLESSED DAUGHTERS AND SONS.
FOR HOLY, YOU SEE-
IS THE REST THAT YOU WILL FIND WITHIN ME.
HOLY AND TRUE-
IS THE REST AND PEACE THAT MY BLOOD OF LIFE GIVES TO BELIEVING YOU.
FOR, HOLY, HOLY, HOLY-
IS THE REST THAT COMES FROM THE SACRED BLOOD OF CHRIST ALMIGHTY.
ETERNAL AND TRUE-
IS THE HOLY BLOOD THAT WAS SHED FOR YOU.
HOLY, YOU SEE-
IS THE GIFT OF BLOOD THAT BRINGS REST TO THOSE WHO FOLLOW ETERNAL ME.
MARCH 24, 2019

MY HOLY BLOOD COVERS THE SOULS OF THE MURDERED AND INNOCENT ONES, SAYS CHRIST JESUS, THE SACRIFICIAL LAMB OF GOD, THE FATHER

CHRIST JESUS, THE SACRIFICIAL LAMB OF GOD, THE FATHER, SPEAKING

MY HOLY PRECIOUS BLOOD-
COVERS THE INNOCENT AND MURDERED SOULS WHOM I WILL ALWAYS TREASURE AND LOVE.
FOR HOLY ARE THEY-
WHO WERE WRONGLY TAKEN AWAY.
MY HOLY INNOCENT ONES WHO WERE TAKEN FROM ME-
NOW, LIVE IN SWEET HEAVEN WITH THE SACRED LIFE SAVING BLOOD OF CHRIST ALMIGHTY.
FOR HOLY, YOU SEE-
ARE THE INNOCENT ONES WHO NEVER GOT THE OPPORTUNITY AND PRIVILEGE TO HONOR AND SERVE LIFE SAVING ME.
HOLY AND TRUE, YOU SEE-
ARE THE INNOCENT AND MURDERED SOULS THAT HAVE BEEN SAVED BY SACRIFICIAL ME.
FOR I DO NOT FORGET, YOU SEE-

THE BLESSED SOULS OF THOSE WHO, WHILE ON EARTH, WERE *TAKEN FROM ME.*
HOLY AND SAVED ARE *THE BLESSED ONES-*
SAFE WITH ME, ARE THE SOULS OF *MY SLAIN AND INNOCENT DAUGHTERS AND SONS.*
FOR *HOLY, YOU SEE-*
IS THE LIFE REWARDING *BLOOD OF CHRIST ALMIGHTY.*
MARCH 24, 2019

IN THE MIDST OF WORLDLY HAVOC, THE PRECIOUS BLOOD OF CHRIST JESUS SEES US THROUGH

<u>BARBARA SPEAKING TO CHRIST JESUS, THE SACRIFICIAL LAMB OF GOD ALMIGHTY</u>

IN THE MIDST OF THE WORLD'S HAVOC AND PAIN, THE BLOOD OF THE SACRIFICIAL LAMB *SEES US THROUGH.*
IN THE MIDST OF SORROW AND GLOOM, WE FOLLOW THE HOLY BLOOD THAT WAS OFFERED BY *SACRIFICIAL YOU.*
FOR *HOLY AND TRUE-*
IS THE PEACE GIVING BLOOD THAT COMES WITH *KNOWING BLESSED AND LIVING SAVING YOU.*
FOR, *HOLY, HOLY, HOLY-*
ARE YOU, *CHRIST ALMIGHTY!*
HOLY AND TRUE-
IS THE SANCTIFYING BLOOD THAT WAS *SHED BY YOU.*
MARCH 24, 2019

PROPHESY TO THEM AGAIN, O BLESSED MESSENGER (BARBARA ANN MARY MACK) OF MY LIVING BLOOD, SAYS CHRIST JESUS, THE SLAUGHTERED LAMB OF GOD

BEHOLD MY PRESENT TESTAMENT

CHRIST JESUS, THE SLAUGHTERED LAMB OF GOD, SPEAKING TO BARBARA, HIS SENT MESSENGER OF DIVINE TRUTH TODAY

PROPHESY! PROPHESY!
FOR MY HOLY MESSAGE, THEY *CANNOT DISPUTE NOR DENY!*
FOR *HOLY AND TRUE*-
ARE THE DIVINE WORDS THAT *I SPEAK THROUGH BLESSED YOU.*
PROPHESY IN *MY HOLY PRESENCE,*
AS YOU TAKE DOWN, IN WRITING, IN YOUR *PEACEFUL EARTHLY RESIDENCE.*
FOR, HOLY AND *RIGHTEOUS, YOU SEE*-
ARE THE WORDS THAT *I SPEAK TO THEE.*
HOLY, ETERNAL AND TRUE-
ARE THE SAYINGS THAT I REVEAL THROUGH *FAITHFUL AND OBEDIENT YOU.*
MARCH 24, 2019

THE PRECIOUS BLOOD OF CHRIST JESUS, THE SLAUGHTERED LAMB OF GOD, WHOM *I WILL ALWAYS TREASURE AND LOVE*

BARBARA SPEAKING

HOLY AND TRUE-
IS THE BLOOD THAT *CLEANSES ME AND YOU.*
HOLY, YOU SEE-
IS THE BLOOD OF *CHRIST ALMIGHTY.*
FOR *CHRIST,* THE SLAUGHTERED LAMB *WHOM I LOVE*-
DESCENDED TO ME FROM THE SWEET *GATES OF HEAVEN ABOVE.*
HOLY, YOU SEE-
IS THE LAMB'S BLOOD THAT *COVERS BLESSED ME.*
HOLY, HOLY, *HOLY, YOU SEE*-
IS THE LAMB'S BLOOD THAT WAS *SHED FOR YOU AND ME.*
FOR, THE PRECIOUS BLOOD OF THE HOLY LAMB WHOM *I WILL ALWAYS LOVE*-
LEADS THE BLESSED ONES THROUGH *HEAVEN'S OPEN GATES ABOVE.*
FOR *HOLY AND TRUE*-
IS THE PRECIOUS BLOOD OF CHRIST JESUS, THAT SURROUNDS AND PROTECTS *WORTHY ME AND YOU.*
MARCH 24, 2019

IT IS A COMPLETION

BARBARA AND HER BEAUTIFUL DAUGHTER AND FRIEND, LA TOYA

IT IS A COMPLETION, SAYS CHRIST JESUS

THE UNIFIED VOICES OF THE BELIEVING ONES SPEAKING

IT IS A COMPLETION-
FOR THE WORLD OF SIN HAS BEEN CONQUERED BY CHRIST ALMIGHTY AND HIS VICTORIOUS CHILDREN.
WE (CHRIST JESUS AND THE BELIEVING ONES) HAVE WON THE FIGHT-
BY CHRIST JESUS' HOLY POWER AND MIGHT.
FOR HOLY IS HE (CHRIST JESUS)-
WHO HAS TAKEN ON THE SINS OF THE NEEDY.
HOLY IS CHRIST JESUS,
THE DIVINE ONE, WHO DESCENDED IN THE MIDST OF SINFUL US.
HOLY AND EVERLASTING IS HE (CHRIST JESUS)-
WHO MADE A GREAT SACRIFICE FOR SINFUL YOU AND ME.

CHRIST, THE VICTORIOUS ONE, SPEAKING

I HAVE COMPLETED MY DIVINE TASK, O WORTHY FRIEND (THE BELIEVING ONE)-
FOR I HAVE BEEN SLAUGHTERED, SO THAT YOU MAY BE FREED FROM SIN.

I WAS BEATEN AND PLACED ON A DEATH TREE,
AS AN EXPRESSION OF MY LOVE FOR THEE.

IT IS A COMPLETION!
IT IS THE DIVINE ASSIGNMENT THAT BRINGS TO AN END, THE SUFFERING OF MY CHILDREN FROM EVERY NATION.
FOR MY SACRIFICE OF DIVINE LOVE-
DESCENDED WITH ME FROM SWEET HEAVEN ABOVE.
HOLY IS MY COMPLETED ASSIGNMENT FROM MY HOLY FATHER GOD-
HOLY IS HIS REALM OF FORGIVENESS AND LOVE.

MARCH 5, 2019

IT IS A COMPLETION, SAYS BARBARA, THE LIVING BRIDE OF CHRIST JESUS, THE SLAUGHTERED LAMB OF GOD

BARBARA SPEAKING TO THE VICTORIOUS CHRIST JESUS

***IT IS A COMPLETION, MY LOVE** (CHRIST JESUS)*,
FOR YOU HAVE BEEN VICTORIOUS OVER THE DIVINE ASSIGNMENT THAT WAS GIVEN TO YOU BY **GOD, OUR HEAVENLY FATHER ABOVE**.
YOU HAVE COMPLETED THE GREAT AND HOLY WORK FOR **OUR LORD GOD;**
AND NOW, YOU WILL FOREVER REIGN IN THE MIDST OF **OUR** (GOD, THE FATHER AND BARBARA) **LOVE**.
HOLY ARE YOU-
COMPLETED IS THE DIVINE ASSIGNMENT OF LOVE THAT YOU WERE **SENT TO DO**.
FOR **GREAT AND HOLY-**
ARE THE COMPLETED WORKS OF **CHRIST ALMIGHTY**.
MARCH 5, 2019

GOD'S GRACE AND MERCY BROUGHT THE BELIEVING ONES TO CHRIST JESUS' LIVING CRUCIFIX

BARBARA SPEAKING

BY GOD'S **DIVINE GRACE AND MERCY-**
WE, THE BELIEVING ONES, ARE LED TO **THE BODY AND BLOOD OF CHRIST, ALMIGHTY**.
CHRIST JESUS, **THE LIVING ONE-**
WHOSE CRUCIFIED BEING LEADS THE CALLED AND CHOSEN TO GOD, THE FATHER'S, **OBEDIENT SACRIFICIAL SON**.
FOR HOLY IS **CHRIST, THE LIVING ONE-**
VICTORIOUS AND SAFE, IS **THE FATHER'S ONLY BEGOTTEN SON**.
HOLY IS HE-
THE **LIVING CHRIST ALMIGHTY**.
FOR, ON **HIS CROSS OF LOVE-**
DESCENDED THE HOLY GIFT OF ETERNAL LIFE AND LOVE, WHO WAS HANGED ON THE HOLY CROSS THAT **DESCENDED FROM HEAVEN ABOVE**.
HOLY IS **TRIUMPHANT HE** (CHRIST JESUS)-
WHO HANGED ON **HIS CROSS OF LOVE FOR ME**.
FOR **GRACE AND MERCY-**

SENT *CHRIST*, THE CRUCIFIED VICTORIOUS ONE, TO **BLESSED YOU AND ME**.
FOR, **HOLY IS HE** (*CHRIST JESUS*)-
WHO SUFFERED FOR BLESSED YOU AND ME ON **SWEET CHOSEN CALVARY**.
MARCH 5, 2019

MY EXECUTION: *OUR EXECUTION, SAYS THE LORD JESUS*

THE EXECUTED LORD JESUS SPEAKING

I WAS EXECUTED FOR YOU, MY CHILDREN.
YES, I, THE *CHRIST*, HAVE PAID THE ULTIMATE PRICE FOR **MY GREAT AND WORTHY CREATION**.
IT WAS **OUR FATHER'S MERCY, YOU SEE**-
THAT GRACED YOU WITH **HOLY SACRIFICIAL ME**.
FOR HOLY IS OUR RIGHTEOUS **GOD AND FATHER ABOVE**.
ETERNAL IS HIS EXPRESSION OF **DIVINE LOVE**.

BARBARA SPEAKING TO THE EXECUTED LORD JESUS

MY LORD *JESUS*-
I HAVE BEEN EXECUTED WITH HE (*CHRIST JESUS*) WHO WAS SENT TO **BLESSED US**.
FOR I TOO WAS **HANGED ON THE HOLY TREE**-
THAT HELD YOUR CRUCIFIED AND **SACRIFICIAL PRECIOUS BODY**.
OUR (*CHRIST JESUS AND BARBARA*) **EXECUTION**-
IS FOR THE SALVATION AND SAFETY OF THOSE FROM **EVERY BLESSED NATION**.
FOR **HOLY AND TRUE**-
ARE **EXECUTED ME AND YOU**.
MARCH 5, 2019

WEEP WITH ME, DEAR BRIDE *(BARBARA)* OF MINE, *SAYS THE SCOURGED AND CRUCIFIED LORD JESUS*

THE SCOURGED AND CRUCIFIED LORD JESUS SPEAKING TO BARBARA, HIS CHOSEN BRIDE

WEEP, WEEP, **WEEP, O BLESSED BRIDE** (*BARBARA*)!

EXHIBIT THE INNER TEARS AND PAIN THAT **YOUR SPIRIT CANNOT HIDE.**
WEEP IN THE **PRESENCE OF OTHERS,**
AS I SAVE YOUR **WORTHY SISTERS AND BROTHERS.**
WEEP WITH ME TODAY-
WEEP, O BLESSED BRIDE OF MINE, AS **YOUR WORTHY SPIRIT AND SOUL BOW AND PRAY.**
WEEP THROUGHOUT **THE BLESSED NIGHT-**
AS YOU KEEP YOUR CRUCIFIED HOLY SPOUSE (CHRIST JESUS) WITHIN **YOUR WORTHY AND BLESSED SIGHT.**
MARCH 5, 2019

WEEP WITH ME, DEAR DAUGHTER (BARBARA), SAYS THE CRUCIFIED LORD JESUS

THE CRUCIFIED LORD JESUS SPEAKING TO BARBARA

WEEP WITH ME, **MY LOVE (BARBARA).**
WEEP WITH ME IN THE HOLY PRESENCE OF **OUR GOD AND FATHER ABOVE.**
FOR **MY SOUL CANNOT BEAR-**
TO ENDURE THE AGONY WITHOUT THE PRESENCE OF **THOSE WHO CARE.**
WEEP WITH ME, O BLESSED **DAUGHTER AND SPOUSE (BARBARA) OF MINE.**
WEEP WITH ME, DEAR ONE, THROUGHOUT THIS **PAINFUL PERIOD OF TIME.**
FOR SATAN, THE DEVIL, HAS UNLEASHED **GREAT PAIN AND SUFFERING-**
INTO THE REALM (EARTH) THAT HOUSES THE CHILDREN OF **CHRIST JESUS, INFINITE KING.**
WEEP WITH ME, MY DAUGHTER,
AS YOU JOIN THE HOLY SPIRIT OF **GOD, OUR HEAVENLY FATHER.**
MARCH 5, 2019

AFTER ALL THESE YEARS, WE, THE BELIEVING ONES, *STILL WEEP AT THE SIGHT AND KNOWLEDGE OF YOUR CRUCIFIXION, LORD* JESUS

BARBARA SPEAKING TO THE VICTORIOUS LORD JESUS

ALTHOUGH IT HAS BEEN **MANY, MANY YEARS-**
WE, THE BELIEVING ONES, STILL WEEP, AT THE SIGHT AND KNOWLEDGE OF **YOUR ABUSE AND TEARS.**
ALTHOUGH THE **YEARS HAVE PAST-**
THE KNOWLEDGE OF YOUR CRUCIFIXION AND SCOURGING, WILL, IN OUR HEARTS AND MINDS, **FOREVER LAST.**
FOR HOLY IS **THE CRUCIFIXION-**
THAT WAS ORDERED BY GOD, THE FATHER, FOR **HIS SINFUL, BUT WORTHY, GREAT CREATION.**
AFTER ALL THESE YEARS, **LORD** JESUS-
WE, THE BELIEVING ONES, ARE GRATEFUL THAT GOD, OUR HOLY FATHER, **GAVE YOU TO SINFUL US.**
FOR **HOLY AND TRUE-**
ARE SACRIFICIAL YOU.
MARCH 5, 2019

CHRIST JESUS' MERCY AND GRACE *LED ME TO THE SACRED PLACE OF SWEET CALVARY*

BARBARA SPEAKING

DIVINE MERCY AND GRACE-
LED ME TO THE PLACE OF JESUS' **CRUCIFIXION AND LIFE SAVING FACE.**
GOD'S DIVINE MERCY-
LED HIS CHILDREN TO **HIS REALM OF ETERNAL GLORY.**
FOR **HOLY AND MERCIFUL IS HE** (CHRIST JESUS)-
WHO WAS HANGED FOR US ON **SWEET CALVARY.**
DIVINE GRACE-
LED ME TO **THE SANCTIFIED PLACE.**
DIVINE MERCY-
LED ME TO THE SCOURGED AND **CRUCIFIED CHRIST ALMIGHTY.**

FOR **MERCIFUL IS HE** (CHRIST JESUS)-
WHO GAVE **HIS PRECIOUS LIFE FOR ME.**
MARCH 5, 2019

AND WE, THE BELIEVING ONES, *WILL WALK WITH JESUS' HOLY TRIUMPHANT CROSS*

BARBARA SPEAKING

WE, THE BELIEVERS, WILL WALK WITH *CHRIST JESUS'* **CROSS OF VICTORY EVERY DAY.**
AS WE FOLLOW THE REWARD OF **HIS HOLY WAY.**
FOR **HOLY IS HE** (CHRIST JESUS)-
WHO HAS GRACED US WITH **HIS VICTORY.**
HOLY IS *THE TRIUMPHANT CROSS*-
THAT HAS RESTORED LIFE AND LOVE TO *THE SPIRITUALLY LOST.*
FOR, **HOLY IS HE** (CHRIST JESUS)-
WHO HAS FOUGHT ***CONTINUOUSLY.***
WE, *THE BELIEVING ONES*-
WILL WALK WITH JESUS, THE FATHER AND GOD OF HIS FAITHFUL AND *VICTORIOUS DAUGHTERS AND SONS.*
HOLY, HOLY, HOLY IS HE (CHRIST JESUS)-
WHOSE HOLY CROSS SITS IN THE MIDST OF VICTORY WITH **YOU AND ME.**
HOLY, HOLY, **HOLY IS THE ONE**-
HOLY, HOLY, HOLY IS *CHRIST* JESUS, **THE FATHER'S VICTORY AND SON!!!**
MARCH 5, 2019

REJOICING IN THE MIDST OF *CHRIST JESUS' VICTORIOUS CROSS OF LOVE*

BARBARA SPEAKING

REJOICE! REJOICE! **REJOICE, O BELIEVING ONES!**
REJOICE IN THE MIDST OF *CHRIST JESUS'* HOLY CROSS, **O BLESSED DAUGHTERS AND SONS!**
FOR **HE IS THE VICTORY-**
WHO HAS WON THE BATTLE OVER SIN AND DEATH, BY **THE POWER OF GOD ALMIGHTY.**
REJOICE! REJOICE!
LET HEAVEN AND EARTH HEAR THE WONDERFUL SOUND OF **YOUR GRATEFUL VOICE!**
FOR **CHRIST, THE TRIUMPHANT SON-**
HAS FULFILLED THE WORKS OF **THE BLESSED ONE** (GOD, THE FATHER).
HOLY, HOLY, **HOLY IS HE-**
HOLY IS **VICTORIOUS CHRIST ALMIGHTY!**
REJOICE, DEAR BROTHERS AND **SISTERS OF MINE!**
REJOICE IN THE MIDST OF THE HOLY CROSS THAT WILL **FOREVER SHINE!**
FOR GREAT AND HOLY IS **THE WORK OF GOD-**
TRIUMPHANT AND WONDERFUL IS **HIS MAGNIFICENT CROSS OF LOVE!!!**
MARCH 5, 2019

OUR *(GOD, THE FATHER, MARY, THE MOTHER OF CHRIST JESUS, AND BARBARA)* FALLING TEARS

GOD, THE FATHER, MARY, THE MOTHER OF CHRIST JESUS, AND BARBARA, SPEAKING

OUR *(GOD, THE FATHER, MARY, THE MOTHER OF CHRIST JESUS, AND BARBARA)* FALLEN TEARS **THAT ARE MANY-**
HAVE COVERED THE BRUISES AND PAIN OF **CHRIST, THE CRUCIFIED ALMIGHTY.**
OUR TEARS OF LOVE-
FELL LIKE WEIGHTLESS FEATHERS FROM **SWEET HEAVEN ABOVE.**
OUR TEARS HAVE COVERED THE WOUNDS OF **CHRIST, OUR HEAVEN SENT LOVE,** AS HE ENDURED THE AFFLICTION AND ABUSE THAT WAS WITNESSED BY HIS HOLY GOD AND FATHER, **IN HEAVEN ABOVE.**
OUR MANY TEARS-

HAVE FLOWED WITH *CHRIST JESUS* AND THE BELIEVING ONES *THROUGH THE YEARS.*
FOR *HOLY ARE THE TEARS-*
THAT HAVE FLOWED WITH HE WHO APPEARED TO HIS LOVED ONES ON EARTH *THROUGH THE YEARS.*
HOLY ARE THE *TEARS OF LOVE-*
THAT JOIN *CHRIST JESUS* AND *HIS HOLY DOVE (SPIRIT).*
FOR *EACH FALLEN TEAR-*
COMES FROM THE HEAVENLY FATHER, MARY, *JESUS'* CHOSEN MOTHER, AND *BARBARA, WHO REALLY CARE.*
HOLY IS THE *SACRIFICIAL CHRIST JESUS-*
EVERLASTING IS THE HOLINESS OF THE *TEARS THAT COME FROM US (GOD, THE FATHER, MARY, AND BARBARA).*
MARCH 5, 2019

CHRIST JESUS: THE EVERLASTING COVENANT *BETWEEN THE BELIEVERS, THE SACRIFICIAL LAMB, AND GOD, THE FATHER*

BARBARA SPEAKING TO GOD, THE FATHER

O HOLY GOD ABOVE-
YOUR BELIEVING FLOCK HAS FOLLOWED *YOUR SACRIFICIAL LAMB'S BLOOD OF DIVINE LOVE.*
WE WILL REMAIN *FAITHFUL AND TRUE,*
FOR WE BELIEVE IN THE *HOLY WORKS THAT YOU DO.*
WE WILL *COMMIT OURSELVES TO YOU,*
FOR YOU ARE THE HOLY ONE WHO *SEES US THROUGH.*
HOLY IS *OUR COVENANT OF LOVE-*
THAT IS GRACED AND BLESSED BY *OUR ORIGIN ABOVE.*
FOR WE, YOUR BELIEVING *CHILDREN TODAY,*
HAVE AGREED TO FOLLOW THE SACRIFICIAL LAMB'S *HOLY LIFE SAVING WAY.*
FOR OUR *ALLEGIANCE IS TO-*
THE HOLY ORIGIN THAT *REVEALS PERFECT YOU.*
WE, YOUR BELIEVING *FLOCK OF LOVE-*
WILL HONOR AND PRAISE OUR *HOLY LORD ABOVE.*
FOR *HOLY IS HE* (CHRIST *JESUS,* THE SACRIFICIAL LAMB OF GOD)-

WHO REVEALS *THE BLESSED TRINITY.*

MARCH 6, 2019

MY PRECIOUS BLOOD COMPLETED IT ALL, *SAYS CHRIST JESUS, THE SACRIFICIAL LAMB OF GOD, THE FATHER*

CHRIST *JESUS,* THE SACRIFICIAL LAMB, SPEAKING

IT IS A COMPLETION-
FOR MY SACRED BLOOD HAS BEEN SHED ON SWEET CALVARY FOR *MY BLESSED CHILDREN.*
FOR, THE GREAT AND HOLY WORK THAT *I HAVE DONE-*
GAVE GLORY AND HONOR TO *MY FATHER'S ONLY BEGOTTEN SACRIFICIAL SON* (CHRIST *JESUS*).
FOR, *HOLY AM I-*
WHO HAVE COMPLETED THE HOLY WORK THAT DESCENDED WITH ME FROM *HEAVEN'S GLORIOUS SKY.*

MARCH 11, 2019

MY COMPLETED WORK FOR GOD ALMIGHTY, IS A LIVING AND EVERLASTING TESTIMONY, *SAYS CHRIST JESUS, THE VICTORIOUS LAMB OF GOD*

CHRIST *JESUS,* THE VICTORIOUS LAMB OF GOD, SPEAKING

THE HOLY WORK THAT I HAVE DONE FOR *GOD, MY FATHER-*
IS A LIVING TESTIMONY TO THOSE WHO LISTEN AND BELIEVE, AS THEY, IN *MY HOLY PRESENCE, GATHER.*
THE COMPLETED WORK THAT I HAVE DONE FOR *GOD, OUR HEAVENLY FATHER-*
DRAWS THOSE WHOM I DIED FOR, *TO ONE ANOTHER.*
FOR, *HOLY IS HE* (GOD, THE FATHER)-
WHO SACRIFICED *BLESSED AND OBEDIENT ME* (CHRIST *JESUS*).

MARCH 11, 2019

THE POWER AND HOLY PRESENCE OF *ALMIGHTY GOD, THE FATHER, AND CHRIST JESUS, THE SACRIFICIAL LAMB OF GOD*

ALMIGHTY GOD, THE FATHER, SPEAKING

I, THE FATHER, AM IN THE MIDST OF **MY SON'S (CHRIST JESUS) PRECIOUS BLOOD.**
I AM IN THE MIDST OF **HIS SACRIFICIAL LOVE.**
FOR, **HOLY IS THE BLOOD**-
THAT WAS SHED FROM **MY SON OF DIVINE LOVE.**
HOLY IS HE (CHRIST JESUS)-
WHO HAS SACRIFICED HIS PRECIOUS LIFE FOR **WORTHY THEE.**
I AM IN THE MIDST OF THE BLOOD THAT SAVES **MY EARTHLY CHILDREN TODAY.**
I AM IN THE MIDST OF THE PRECIOUS BLOOD THAT LEADS ALL TO **MY SON'S (CHRIST JESUS) LIFE SAVING HOLY WAY.**
FOR **HOLY IS THE WAY**-
THAT LEADS TO **MY HEAVENLY KINGDOM TODAY.**
HOLY IS HE (CHRIST JESUS)-
WHO SAVES THOSE WHO FOLLOW THE LIFE SAVING BLOOD OF **CHRIST ALMIGHTY.**
 MARCH 12, 2019

MY SHEEP AND ME, *SAYS THE LORD JESUS*

THE SACRIFICIAL LAMB OF GOD AND HIS SHEEP

THE SACRIFICIAL LAMB OF GOD SPEAKING

MY SHEEP *FOLLOW ME EVERY DAY*-
FOR THEY ARE EAGER TO LEARN OF *MY HOLY LIFE SAVING WAY.*
FOR *HOLY AND TRUE*-
IS THE SACRIFICIAL LAMB (CHRIST JESUS) WHO *DIED FOR YOU.*
HOLY, YOU SEE-
ARE MY SHEEP WHO *FOLLOW SACRIFICIAL ME.*
MY SHEEP LISTEN FOR MY REJOICING VOICE *THROUGHOUT EACH DAY*-
AS THEY SEEK GOD'S HEAVENLY KINGDOM AND *MY HOLY LIFE SAVING WAY.*
FOR, HOLY, HOLY, *HOLY AND TRUE*-
IS THE BLOOD OF LIFE THAT WAS *SHED FOR BLESSED YOU.*

MARCH 22, 2019

THE SHEEP THAT *FOLLOW THE LAMB OF GOD*

CHRIST JESUS, THE LAMB OF GOD, SPEAKING

MY SHEEP HEAR MY HOLY CALL, AND *THEY FOLLOW ME.*
MY SHEEP HEAR MY CALL, AND THEY FOLLOW THE HOLY VOICE OF *THE SACRIFICIAL LAMB OF GOD ALMIGHTY.*
FOR *HOLY ARE THEY*-
WHO FOLLOW THE SACRIFICIAL *LAMB'S LIFE SAVING WAY.*
HOLY AND TRUE-
ARE THE SHEEP THAT *LISTEN TOO.*
FOR THEY TRULY *KNOW AND HONOR ME*-
THEY HONOR THE HOLY VOICE OF *CHRIST ALMIGHTY.*
FOR, *HOLY AND EVERLASTING*-
IS THE VOICE OF CHRIST JESUS, *THE SACRIFICIAL LAMB AND KING.*
HOLY AND TRUE-
ARE THE BLESSED ONES WHO SEEK *THE GOOD WORKS THAT I DO.*

MARCH 22, 2019

THE SHEEP: MY SHEEP WHO HAVE GONE ASTRAY, SAYS CHRIST JESUS, THE LEADING LAMB OF GOD, THE FATHER

CHRIST JESUS, THE LEADING LAMB OF GOD, THE FATHER, SPEAKING TO HIS LOST SHEEP TODAY

WHY HAVE YOU ABANDON ME?
WHY HAVE YOU LEFT THE COMFORT OF THE LIVING BLOOD THAT HAS *CARED FOR THEE?*
WHY HAVE YOU *FORSAKEN ME?*
WHY HAVE YOU LEFT THE *LOVED THAT CREATED THEE?*
FOR *HOLY AND TRUE-*
IS THE LOVE OF THE BLOOD THAT WAS *SHED FOR YOUR CHILDREN AND YOU.*
WHY? WHY? WHY?
WHY DO YOU *OPENLY DENY?*
WHY DO YOU DENY-
THE HOLY ONE (CHRIST JESUS) WHO DESCENDED TO YOU FROM *ABOVE THE HEAVENLY SKY?*
FOR, *CAN YOU NOT SEE-*
THE TRUE LOVE AND GRACE OF *CHRIST, THE SACRIFICIAL GOD ALMIGHTY?*
FOR *HOLY AND TRUE-*
IS THE BLOOD OF CHRIST THAT *DESCENDED IN THE MIDST OF YOU.*
FOR *HOLY AND TRUE-*
IS THE GOOD SHEPHERD (CHRIST JESUS) WHO *SEEKS ALL OF YOU.*
WHY? WHY? WHY-
DO YOU CAUSE YOUR GREAT CREATOR TO *WEEP AND CRY?*
FOR *CAN YOU NOT SEE-*
THE TEARS THAT FALL FROM THE HOLY ESSENCE OF *CHRIST ALMIGHTY?*
OH WANDERING SHEEP-
WHY DO YOU CAUSE THE SACRIFICIAL *LAMB OF GOD TO WEEP?*

MARCH 23, 2019

MY WORTHY FOLD: MY EARTHLY AND HEAVENLY POT OF NON-PERISHING GOLD, SAYS CHRIST JESUS, THE LAMB OF THE LIVING GOD, THE FATHER

CHRIST JESUS, THE LAMB OF GOD, THE FATHER, SPEAKING TO HIS HOLY SHEEP TODAY

MY WORTHY FOLD-
O HEAVENLY POT OF GOLD-
I WANT YOU TO KNOW-
THAT I, THE SACRIFICIAL BLOOD OF LIFE, AM WITH YOU WHEREVER YOU *WANDER AND GO.*
FOR *I, YOUR LORD AND GOD,*
HAVE GRACED YOU WITH *MY REALM OF UNENDING LOVE.*
FOR *HOLY AND TRUE-*
IS THE GOOD SHEPHERD WHO *LEADS TRUSTING AND OBEDIENT YOU.*
HOLY AND ETERNAL, *YOU SEE-*
IS YOUR FAITHFUL *GOD, THE ALMIGHTY.*
FOR *HOLY AND TRUE-*
IS THE POT OF *NON-PERISHING* GOLD THAT I CALL *BLESSED AND SAVED YOU.*

MARCH 23, 2019

FOLLOW ME

CHRIST JESUS, THE UNBLEMISHED LAMB OF GOD, THE FATHER, SPEAKING

FOLLOW ME-
ALL WHO DESIRE TO LIVE IN SWEET PARADISE WITH ***BLESSED ME; CHRIST ALMIGHTY.***
FOLLOW ME, DEAR *LAMBS*, THROUGH THE ***OPEN GATE.***
FOLLOW ME, DEAR *SHEEP*, FOR YOUR BLESSED SOULS ***NO LONGER HAVE TO WAIT.***
FOR ***WITHIN HOLY ME-***
YOU WILL DINE IN THE REALM OF ***SWEET EVERLASTING PEACE AND TRANQUILITY.***
COME, COME, COME-
FOR YOU ARE ***TRULY WELCOME!***
COME, O ***BLESSED SHEEP,***

SO THAT YOUR TROUBLED SOULS WILL *NO LONGER WEEP.*
COME UNTO *ME TODAY,*
SO THAT I MAY LEAD YOU TO *MY GREAT AND HOLY WAY.*
COME OVER HERE-
SO THAT YOU MAY WITNESS THE LOVE OF *HE (CHRIST JESUS) WHO DOES CARE.*
COME TO ME-
AND FOLLOW THE SACRIFICIAL LAMB; *CHRIST JESUS, THE ALMIGHTY.*
FOR *HOLY AND TRUE-*
ARE THE WORDS THAT *CALL OBEDIENT YOU.*
HOLY, YOU SEE-
ARE THE PRECIOUS LITTLE LAMBS WHO ARE *CALLED AND BLESSED BY ME.*
MARCH 25, 2019

THE BLESSED LAMBS AND SHEEP WHO FOLLOW CHRIST JESUS, THE SENT AND VICTORIOUS LAMB OF GOD

CHRIST *JESUS,* THE SENT AND VICTORIOUS LAMB OF GOD, SPEAKING

THOSE WHO *FOLLOW ME-*
WILL ENTER THE *GATES OF SWEET ETERNITY.*
FOR *I, THE SENT AND HOLY LAMB-*
CAME FROM THE HOLY ESSENCE OF *GOD, THE FATHER, YES, THE GREAT AND INFINITE I AM.*
FOR *HOLY AND TRUE-*
IS THE SACRIFICIAL LAMB WHO *CALLS AND LEADS BLESSED YOU.*
COME WITH ME-
THE HOLY LAMB OF GOD, WHO *LEADS BLESSED THEE.*
FOLLOW ME, O PRECIOUS *LAMBS WHOM I LOVE.*
COME, O BLESSED LAMBS, AS I LEAD YOU TO *MY HEAVENLY FOLD ABOVE.*
FOR *HOLY, YOU SEE-*
ARE THE PRECIOUS LAMBS WHO ARE *CALLED BY SACRIFICIAL SENT ME.*
HOLY, YOU SEE-

ARE THE BLESSED SHEEP WHO ENTER *HEAVEN'S OPEN GATES WITH ME.*
HOLY AND TRUE-
ARE THE GATES THAT *I WILL LEAD YOU THROUGH.*
FOR IT IS REAL-
THE HOLY LOVE FOR YOU THAT *THE FATHER AND I FEEL!*
MARCH 25, 2019

BEHOLD MY PRESENT TESTAMENT

I HAVE COME TO FEED MY SHEEP, SAYS CHRIST JESUS, THE RISEN LAMB OF GOD

CHRIST *JESUS*, THE RISEN LAMB OF GOD, SPEAKING

I HAVE COME BACK *TO FEED-*
MY BLESSED FLOCK OF LOVE WHO ARE *IN NEED.*
I HAVE COME, *YOU SEE-*
SO THAT MY WORTHY FOLD WILL *FOLLOW ME.*
I HAVE COME IN THEIR *HOLY PRESENCE,*
AS I DELIVER MY WORDS OF TRUTH TO *BARBARA,* IN HER *EARTHLY RESIDENCE.*
I HAVE COME, *YOU SEE-*
SO THAT YOU MAY *BELIEVE IN ME.*
FOR *HOLY AND TRUE-*
ARE THE WORDS OF LIFE AND LOVE THAT *I REVEAL TO YOU.*
 FOR *HOLY YOU SEE-*

are the blessings that come with *FOLLOWING AND KNOWING SACRIFICIAL ME.*
I have come to *FEED YOU TODAY,*
as you learn of *MY HOLY LIFE SAVING WAY.*
For *HOLY, HOLY, HOLY-*
is *THE SACRIFICIAL CHRIST ALMIGHTY.*
March 25, 2019

ENTER MY LIVING BLOOD, *SAYS CHRIST JESUS*

In the midst of your suffering, I will comfort your holy blood that was shed for us, Lord Jesus,

Barbara speaking to the wounded Lord Jesus

In the midst of your abuse and suffering, I will comfort your holy blood that was *shed for us,*
O sacrificial Lord Jesus.
I will *comfort the blood–*
that flowed from *your wounds of divine love.*
I will comfort, *you see–*
the holy blood that was shed for *blessed sanctified me.*
For *holy is the blood–*
that flowed from our *Lord and God of love.*
Holy is his precious blood, *you see–*
for it, the precious blood of *Christ Jesus,* was shed to *save blessed me.*
March 5, 2019

The holy arms and spirit that comfort the blood of Christ Jesus, God's sacrificial Lamb of divine love and mercy.

Barbara speaking

My wounded arms of love have surrounded the beloved spirit of *Christ Jesus, the Father's sacrificial Lamb of love.*
My wounded spirit has united with my *heavenly God and Father above.*
Weep, weep, weep, *O blessed arms and spirit of mine.*
Weep in the holy presence of the Father's wounded Lamb, throughout this period of *unholy people and time.*
I have surrounded the flowing blood of *Christ Jesus, God's sacrificial Lamb of love,*
as my spirit united with the *tears of our heavenly Father above.*
For holy is the *flowing sacrificial blood–*
that comes from the holy throne of the mighty King *(Almighty God, the Father)* who *sits in sweet heaven above.*
My blessed *arms of love–*

COMFORT THE BLOOD OF THE HOLY ONE *(CHRIST JESUS)* WHO DESCENDED FROM THE *HEAVENLY GATES ABOVE.*
MY WEEPING SPIRIT-
RELEASES A SOUND OF COMFORT TO THE BLOOD OF *CHRIST JESUS*, SO THAT THE WORLD MAY *BOW AS THEY HEAR IT.*
WEEP! WEEP! WEEP, O BLESSED *ARMS AND SPIRIT OF MINE!*
WEEP IN THE HOLY PRESENCE OF GOD'S FLOWING LIFE SAVING BLOOD, THROUGHOUT THE REALM OF *THIS BLESSED PERIOD OF SALVATION AND TIME.*
MARCH 7, 2019

THE HOLY BLOOD THAT WAS *SHED FOR YOU AND ME*

BARBARA SPEAKING TO *JESUS'* HOLY BLOOD

O HOLY BLOOD THAT WAS *SHED FOR ME-*
I BOW IN THE PRESENCE OF *CHRIST JESUS, THE LIVING SACRIFICIAL KING AND ALMIGHTY.*
O HOLY BLOOD THAT FLOWS THROUGH THE VEINS OF *CHRIST JESUS, MY VICTORIOUS GOD AND KING OF KINGS-*
I THANK YOU FOR FLOWING IN THE MIDST OF THE BELIEVING ONES AS WE LIFT OUR BLESSED AND UNIFIED *SPIRIT THAT SINGS.*
HOLY IS THE FLOWING *BLOOD OF CHRIST JESUS-*
HOLY IS THE ROYAL DIVINE BLOOD THAT FLOWS IN THE MIDST OF *BLESSED AND WORTHY US.*
HOLY, HOLY, HOLY-
IS THE FLOWING LIFE REWARDING BLOOD OF *CHRIST ALMIGHTY.*
MARCH 7, 2019

LIFT ME UP ON HIGH, O PRECIOUS BLOOD OF *CHRIST JESUS, GOD'S SLAUGHTERED LAMB*

BARBARA SPEAKING OF THE BLOOD OF CHRIST *JESUS,* THE SACRIFICIAL LAMB OF GOD

LIFT MY BLESSED SPIRIT UP,

SO THAT I MAY DRINK THE LIFE SAVING BLOOD THAT *FLOWS THROUGH CHRIST JESUS' HOLY CUP.*
FOR HOLY AND EVER-FLOWING IS *THE BLOOD OF DIVINE LOVE-*
THAT FLOWS FROM THE REALM THAT WAITS FOR US IN *SWEET PARADISE ABOVE.*
LIFT ME UP-
SO THAT I MAY REACH THE PURITY OF *CHRIST JESUS' HOLY CUP.*
FOR *HOLY IS THE BLOOD-*
THAT FLOWS FROM THE SPIRIT AND BODY OF *CHRIST, OUR HOLY GOD OF LOVE.*
LIFT ME HIGH-
ABOVE *THE BRIGHT BLUE SKY-*
FOR HOLY IS *THE BLOOD OF LIFE-*
THAT WAS SHED FOR ME, THE *CRUCIFIED LAMB'S EVERLASTING FRIEND AND WIFE.*
LIFT ME UP HIGH, SO THAT *I MAY SEE-*
THE HOLY BLOOD THAT WAS *SHED FOR WORTHY ME.*
LIFT ME UP HIGH-
SO THAT I MAY REJOICE IN THE MIDST OF THE LIFE SAVING BLOOD THAT WAS *SHED FOR YOU AND I.*

MARCH 7, 2019

THE BRILLIANT LIGHT THAT SHINES FROM THE PRECIOUS BLOOD OF *CHRIST JESUS, THE SLAUGHTERED SACRIFICIAL LAMB OF GOD ALMIGHTY*

BARBARA SPEAKING

I WILL BATHE IN THE BRILLIANT LIGHT OF *THE PRECIOUS BLOOD OF CHRIST JESUS.*
I WILL BATHE WITHIN THE HEAVEN SENT LOVE THAT *COVERS BELIEVING US.*
FOR, HOLY IS *THE BRILLIANT LIGHT OF LOVE-*
THAT COMES FROM *CHRIST JESUS' PRECIOUS BLOOD.*
I WILL CLING TO THE BLOOD OF *LIFE, LOVE AND LIGHT-*
THAT SHINES OVER THE BLESSED ONES *THROUGHOUT THE NIGHT.*
FOR, HOLY, HOLY, *HOLY IS THE BRILLIANT LIGHT-*
THAT COMES FROM THE SACRED BLOOD OF *CHRIST JESUS' HOLY MIGHT.*

MARCH 8, 2019

THE POWER OF MY HOLY BLOOD REJOICES WITH MY BELIEVING CHILDREN TODAY, SAYS CHRIST JESUS, THE SACRIFICIAL LAMB OF ALMIGHTY GOD, THE LIVING FATHER

CHRIST JESUS, THE SACRIFICIAL LAMB OF ALMIGHTY GOD, THE LIVING FATHER, SPEAKING

REJOICE! REJOICE! **REJOICE WITH ME!**
REJOICE WITH MY FLOWING BLOOD, AS IT **SANCTIFIES BLESSED THEE!**
FOR **HOLY AND TRUE-**
IS THE LIVING BLOOD THAT SURROUNDS BELOVED AND **BLESSED YOU.**
HOLY AND TRUE-
IS THE LIVING BLOOD THAT HAS **RESCUED TORMENTED YOU.**
FOR YOU HAVE BEEN RESCUED FROM **SATAN'S WORLD OF DESTRUCTION AND SIN.**
MY HOLY BLOOD OF LIFE HAS RESCUED YOU, **O WORTHY AND GRATEFUL FRIEND.**
REJOICE IN THE MIDST OF **SACRED LOVE!**
REJOICE WITHIN THE COMFORT OF **MY LIVING FLOWING BLOOD.**
FOR IT IS THE SOURCE OF LIFE, **DEAR ONES.**
IT TRULY SUSTAINS MY WORTHY AND WELL-LOVED **DAUGHTERS AND SONS.**
FOR **SACRED AND TRUE-**
IS THE BLOOD THAT **SAVES BLESSED YOU.**

MARCH 9, 2019

THE HOLINESS OF MY LIVING BLOOD, SAYS THE LORD JESUS

THE LORD JESUS SPEAKING

THE HOLINESS OF MY FLOWING BLOOD HAS **TRAVELED THROUGH THE YEARS.**
IT HAS COVERED THE SPIRITS AND SOULS OF THOSE WHO HAVE **SHED MANY TEARS.**
THE HOLINESS OF MY LIVING BLOOD HAS **COMFORTED THE MEEK-**
IT HAS GIVEN EVERLASTING LIFE TO **THE STRONG AND THE WEAK.**
HOLY IS **MY FLOWING BLOOD-**
ETERNAL IS **THE SACRIFICIAL LAMB OF GOD.**
FOR MY HOLY BLOOD IS **FOR THE LIVING,**
FOR THEY DO HONOR AND FOLLOW **CHRIST, THE KING.**

BARBARA ANN MARY MACK

HOLY, HOLY, HOLY,
IS THE LIVING FLOWING BLOOD OF *CHRIST ALMIGHTY.*
MARCH 9, 2019

DIVINE ECSTASY AND BLISS COME FROM THE PRECIOUS BLOOD OF CHRIST JESUS, THE SACRIFICIAL LAMB OF GOD, THE FATHER

BARBARA SPEAKING

HAPPINESS AND *LIFE GIVING BLISS-*
FLOW FROM THE PRECIOUS BLOOD AND *THE SACRIFICIAL LAMB'S HOLY KISS.*
DIVINE JOY AND *SPIRITUAL ECSTASY-*
FLOW FROM THE *SACRED BLOOD OF CHRIST ALMIGHTY.*
THE SPIRITUAL *BLISS AND JOY-*
COVER THE SOULS OF THE *BELIEVING LITTLE GIRL AND BOY.*
FOR HOLY IS *CHRIST JESUS' FLOWING BLOOD OF LOVE-*
THAT DESCENDS TO THE BELIEVING ONES FROM *SWEET HEAVEN ABOVE.*
HOLY IS HE (CHRIST *JESUS*)-
WHO HAS SHED HIS PRECIOUS LIFE SAVING BLOOD FOR YOU AND ME.
HOLY, HOLY, HOLY-
IS THE BLOOD THAT RELEASES DIVINE LOVE, GLADNESS, AND *SPIRITUAL ECSTASY.*
MARCH 12, 2019

BY THE POWER OF YOUR HOLY UNDEFEATED BLOOD, WE DID IT AGAIN, LORD JESUS

BARBARA SPEAKING TO THE VICTORIOUS SACRIFICIAL LAMB OF GOD

WE DID IT AGAIN, O HOLY ONE!
WE COMPLETED OUR DIVINE ASSIGNMENT THAT WAS GIVEN TO ME, BY *ALMIGHTY GOD'S SACRIFICIAL SON* (CHRIST *JESUS*)!
I COMPLETED THE BLESSED ASSIGNMENT THAT WAS *GIVEN TO ME-*
WITH THE AID AND GUIDANCE OF *CHRIST ALMIGHTY.*
I COMPLETED ANOTHER *DIVINE BOOK OF LOVE,*
WHICH INCLUDED MANY MESSAGES FROM *SWEET HEAVEN ABOVE.*

THE MESSAGES WERE VERY *CARING AND SWEET,*
FOR THEY WERE FOR THOSE, THROUGH YOU, WHOM *I WOULD GREET.*
THEY WERE WORDS OF HOPE AND LOVE FROM *THE LORD OUR GOD-*
THAT DESCENDED FROM GOD, THE FATHER'S, *REALM OF CONTINUOUS LOVE.*
ALTHOUGH SATAN, THE DEVIL, *TRIED TO PREVENT ME-*
FROM SHARING THE GOOD NEWS THAT *DESCENDED FROM THEE.*
WITH *YOUR VICTORY AND MIGHT-*
YOU REMOVED SATAN'S UNWANTED STENCH *FROM MY SIGHT.*
BECAUSE OF YOUR *DIVINE POWER AND GREATNESS-*
MANY WILL BECOME *YOUR CHOSEN WITNESSES.*
FOR *HOLY ARE YOU-*
WHO HAVE SEEN ANOTHER *DIVINE BOOK OF LOVE THROUGH.*
I NOW REJOICE IN *YOUR HOLY PRESENCE,*
AS I PROCEED IN ANOTHER HOLY WORK FOR YOU IN *MY HUMBLE RESIDENCE.*
FOR *HOLY AND TRUE-*
ARE ETERNAL AND *LIFE REWARDING YOU.*
MARCH 14, 2019

WE DID IT AGAIN, LORD *JESUS! OH WHAT A TEAM (ALMIGHTY GOD, THE BLESSED TRINITY AND BARBARA)!*

BARBARA SPEAKING TO THE LORD *JESUS*

OH WHAT A *TRIUMPHANT TEAM, LORD JESUS!*
YOU, O HOLY ONE, HAVE TRIUMPHED AGAIN IN THE PRESENCE OF *BLESSED US.*
YOU HAVE DEFEATED THOSE WHO HAVE *TRIED TO PREVENT-*
THE HOLY BLESSINGS THAT *THROUGH ME WERE SENT.*
FOR WITHIN THE *DIVINE WRITING-*
REVEALS THE HOLY PRESENCE OF *GOD, OUR EVERLASTING KING.*
BECAUSE OF *HOLY YOU-*
MY GOD INSPIRED BOOK *CAME THROUGH.*
I DID NOT LET *ANYTHING OR ONE PREVENT-*
THE PUBLICATION OF THE HOLY WRITINGS THAT THROUGH ME, *YOU HAVE SENT.*
FOR *HOLY AND TRUE-*
ARE THE DIVINE WORDS THAT COME FROM *BLESSED YOU.*
OH WHAT A *GREAT TEAM WE ARE-*

FOR YOUR HOLY WORDS AND SAYINGS HAVE *TRAVELED VERY FAR.*
YOUR WORDS OF LOVE-
DESCENDS TO ME FROM *SWEET HEAVEN ABOVE.*
I WILL CONTINUE-
TO WRITE THE HOLY MESSAGES AND SAYINGS THAT COME FROM *BLESSED LIFE SAVING YOU.*
MARCH 14, 2019

IF I DID NOT HAVE THE LIVING BLOOD OF *CHRIST JESUS,* THE SACRIFICIAL LAMB OF GOD, WITHIN ME, *WHERE WOULD I BE?*

BARBARA SPEAKING

IF I DID NOT HAVE THE LIVING BLOOD OF *CHRIST JESUS* WITHIN ME-
I WOULD NOT BE IN CONTROL OF MY *MIND AND VULNERABLE BODY.*
IF I DID NOT HAVE *THE LIVING BLOOD-*
THAT DESCENDS FROM *THE LAMB'S HEAVENLY REALM ABOVE-*
I COULD NOT BE-
WRAPPED WITHIN THE LOVE AND SECURITY OF *CHRIST ALMIGHTY.*
IF I-
DID NOT HAVE THE PRECIOUS BLOOD THAT THE *UNBELIEVERS DENY-*
WHERE WOULD I BE? WHERE WOULD I BE? *WHERE WOULD I BE-*
WITHOUT THE SACRIFICED ONE'S *(CHRIST JESUS)* BLOOD THAT *COMFORTS AND LEADS BLESSED ME?*
IF I DID NOT HAVE *THE LAMB'S GIFT OF LIFE-*
I WOULD NO LONGER BE *HIS CHOSEN FRIEND AND WIFE.*
FOR *I COULD NOT IMAGINE-*
LIVING WITHOUT THE PRECIOUS BLOOD OF *CHRIST JESUS, MY SACRIFICIAL LORD, GOD, AND EVERLASTING FRIEND.*
FOR, *HOLY IS THE BLOOD-*
THAT FLOWED FROM *MY HOLY GOD OF LOVE.*

BARBARA SPEAKING TO CHRIST JESUS

MY **HOLY LORD AND GOD-**
I COULD NEVER IMAGING LIVING WITHOUT **YOUR FLOWING LIFE SAVING BLOOD.**
FOR **HOLY IS THE BLOOD-**
THAT WAS SHED FROM THE BODY OF HE (CHRIST JESUS) WHOM **I WILL ALWAYS FOLLOW, WORSHIP AND LOVE.**
MARCH 15, 2019

O HOLY PRECIOUS BLOOD OF CHRIST JESUS; WHERE WOULD I BE WITHOUT THE PRESENCE OF LIFE GIVING THEE?

BARBARA SPEAKING

WHERE WOULD I BE? **WHERE WOULD I BE-**
WITHOUT THE BLOOD THAT GIVES **EVERLASTING LIFE TO ME?**
I WOULD BE-
LOST AND WANDERING, **YOU SEE.**
FOR THERE IS **NOT A LIFE-**
OTHER THAN BEING THE **SACRIFICIAL LAMB'S CHOSEN WIFE.**
FOR **HOLY IS HE** (CHRIST JESUS)-
WHO SHED HIS PRECIOUS **BLOOD FOR ME.**
I AM **COMFORTED WITHIN-**
THE HOLY BLOOD OF CHRIST JESUS, MY ETERNAL **GOD, SPOUSE AND FRIEND.**
I WOULD BE **LOST, YOU SEE-**
WITHOUT THE LIVING BLOOD THAT HAS SANCTIFIED AND SAVED **BLESSED SENT ME.**
WHERE WOULD I BE? **WHERE WOULD I BE-**
WITHOUT THE LIVING BLOOD OF **CHRIST ALMIGHTY?**
MARCH 15, 2019

SAVED BY THE POWER OF MY HOLY BLOOD, *SAYS CHRIST JESUS*

IN THE MIDST OF YOUR SUFFERING, *I WILL COMFORT YOUR HOLY BLOOD THAT WAS SHED FOR US, LORD JESUS,*

BARBARA SPEAKING TO THE WOUNDED LORD JESUS

IN THE MIDST OF YOUR ABUSE AND SUFFERING, I WILL COMFORT YOUR HOLY BLOOD THAT WAS **SHED FOR US,**
O SACRIFICIAL LORD JESUS.
I WILL **COMFORT THE BLOOD-**
THAT FLOWED FROM **YOUR WOUNDS OF DIVINE LOVE.**
I WILL COMFORT, **YOU SEE-**
THE HOLY BLOOD THAT WAS SHED FOR **BLESSED SANCTIFIED ME.**
FOR **HOLY IS THE BLOOD-**

THAT FLOWED FROM OUR **LORD AND GOD OF LOVE.**
HOLY IS HIS PRECIOUS BLOOD, **YOU SEE-**
FOR IT, THE PRECIOUS BLOOD OF *CHRIST JESUS,* WAS SHED TO **SAVE BLESSED ME.**
MARCH 5, 2019

THE HOLY BLOOD THAT WAS *SHED FOR YOU AND ME*

BARBARA SPEAKING TO *JESUS'* HOLY BLOOD

O HOLY BLOOD THAT WAS **SHED FOR ME-**
I BOW IN THE PRESENCE OF *CHRIST JESUS,* **THE LIVING SACRIFICIAL KING AND ALMIGHTY.**
O HOLY BLOOD THAT FLOWS THROUGH THE VEINS OF *CHRIST JESUS,* **MY *VICTORIOUS GOD AND KING OF KINGS*-**
I THANK YOU FOR FLOWING IN THE MIDST OF THE BELIEVING ONES AS WE LIFT OUR BLESSED AND UNIFIED **SPIRIT THAT SINGS.**
HOLY IS THE FLOWING **BLOOD OF CHRIST *JESUS*-**
HOLY IS THE ROYAL DIVINE BLOOD THAT FLOWS IN THE MIDST OF **BLESSED AND WORTHY US.**
HOLY, HOLY, HOLY-
IS THE FLOWING LIFE REWARDING BLOOD OF **CHRIST ALMIGHTY.**
MARCH 7, 2019

LIFT ME UP ON HIGH, O PRECIOUS BLOOD OF *CHRIST JESUS, GOD'S SLAUGHTERED LAMB*

BARBARA SPEAKING OF THE BLOOD OF CHRIST *JESUS,* THE SACRIFICIAL LAMB OF GOD

LIFT MY BLESSED SPIRIT UP,
SO THAT I MAY DRINK THE LIFE SAVING BLOOD THAT ***FLOWS THROUGH CHRIST JESUS'* HOLY CUP.**
FOR HOLY AND EVER-FLOWING IS *THE BLOOD OF DIVINE LOVE-*
THAT FLOWS FROM THE REALM THAT WAITS FOR US IN *SWEET PARADISE ABOVE.*
LIFT ME UP-

SO THAT I MAY REACH THE PURITY OF CHRIST JESUS' HOLY CUP.
FOR HOLY IS THE BLOOD-
THAT FLOWS FROM THE SPIRIT AND BODY OF CHRIST, OUR HOLY GOD OF LOVE.
LIFT ME HIGH-
ABOVE THE BRIGHT BLUE SKY-
FOR HOLY IS THE BLOOD OF LIFE-
THAT WAS SHED FOR ME, THE CRUCIFIED LAMB'S EVERLASTING FRIEND AND WIFE.
LIFT ME UP HIGH, SO THAT I MAY SEE-
THE HOLY BLOOD THAT WAS SHED FOR WORTHY ME.
LIFT ME UP HIGH-
SO THAT I MAY REJOICE IN THE MIDST OF THE LIFE SAVING BLOOD THAT WAS SHED FOR YOU AND I.
MARCH 7, 2019

THE PRECIOUS AND PRICELESS BLOOD OF CHRIST JESUS, THE SCOURGED AND CRUCIFIED ONE

BARBARA SPEAKING

THE PRECIOUS AND PRICELESS BLOOD OF CHRIST JESUS-
WAS SHED, SO THAT IT MAY REDEEM BLESSED AND REPENTANT US.
THE PRICELESS BLOOD OF THE LAMB OF GOD, OUR HOLY FATHER-
SAVES THE SOULS OF MY REPENTANT SISTER AND BROTHER.
CHRIST JESUS' PRICELESS BLOOD-
REVEALS THE SACRED ENTRANCE TO ALMIGHTY GOD'S REALM OF CONTINUOUS UNCONDITIONAL LOVE.
THE PRICELESS BLOOD OF DIVINE LOVE-
LEADS US TO JESUS' ORIGIN AND HOME ABOVE.
HOLY IS THE PRECIOUS BLOOD OF THE SLAUGHTERED LAMB OF LOVE.
ETERNAL IS THE BLESSED SPIRIT OF HE (CHRIST JESUS) WHO IS KING ON EARTH AND IN SWEET HEAVEN ABOVE.
HOLY IS THE PRICELESS BLOOD OF HE (CHRIST JESUS)-
WHO HAS DIED FOR US ON SWEET CALVARY.
HOLY, HOLY, HOLY-
IS CHRIST JESUS, THE EVERLASTING KING AND ALMIGHTY!

MARCH 6, 2019

CHRIST JESUS, THE PRICELESS LOVE

BARBARA SPEAKING

LET US, THE BELIEVING ONES, GIVE PRAISE, GLORY AND HONOR TO **CHRIST JESUS, THE HOLY REALM OF PRICELESS LOVE.**
LET US, DEAR SISTERS AND BROTHERS, GIVE HONOR AND RECOGNITION, TO THE HOLY ONE WHO **DESCENDED FROM SWEET HEAVEN ABOVE.**
FOR HOLY IS **CHRIST JESUS, THE PRICELESS SON**-
WHOSE BATTLES AGAINST THE REALM OF EVIL AND DESTRUCTION, **HE HAS ALREADY WON.**
FOR **HIS MIGHT AND GLORY**-
HAVE CONQUER THE EVIL REALM THAT HAS CREPT INTO **HIS LIFE SAVING HOLY STORY.**
HOLY IS HE (CHRIST JESUS)-
WHO HAS SAVED AND BLESSED THE REPENTANT ONES AND **THE WORTHY.**

MARCH 6, 2019

THE HOLY AND PURELY DIVINE BLOOD THAT WAS SHED FOR ME AND MY BELIEVING GOD SENT FAMILY

BARBARA SPEAKING TO THE PRECIOUS BLOOD OF CHRIST JESUS

O HOLY BLOOD THAT WAS **SHED FOR ME.**
I PRAISE YOU FOR FLOWING FROM THE HOLY BEING OF **CHRIST JESUS, THE ALMIGHTY.**
I PRAISE AND **THANK THEE**-
FOR EXITING THE HOLY BODY OF **GOD ALMIGHTY** (CHRIST JESUS).
I ADORE YOU, O PRECIOUS FLOWING BLOOD OF **CHRIST, OUR SACRIFICIAL KING.**
I PRAISE YOU FOR COMPLETING THAT **WONDERFUL SACRIFICIAL AND VICTORIOUS THING** (JESUS' CRUCIFIXION).
O HOLY FLOWING BLOOD OF **CHRIST, THE EVERLASTING KING**-
I WILL JOIN YOUR HOLY CHOIRS AS THEY **LIFT UP THEIR VOICES AND SING.**
O HOLY BLOOD OF **GOD'S SLAUGHTERED LAMB OF LOVE** (CHRIST JESUS)-

I PRAISE AND THANK YOU, FOR DESCENDING FROM THE *HEAVENLY GATES ABOVE*.
HOLY IS THE *FLOWING BLOOD*-
HOLY IS THE LIFE SUSTAINING GIFT (*JESUS' FLOWING BLOOD*) THAT DESCENDED TO US WITH *UNENDING MERCY AND LOVE*.
HOLY IS THE BLOOD THAT FLOWS FROM THE BEING OF THE WOUNDED LORD *JESUS, FOR BLESSED ME*.
HOLY IS THE FLOWING FOOD (*JESUS' FLOWING BLOOD*) THAT COMES FROM LIFE GIVING *CHRIST ALMIGHTY*.
HOLY, HOLY, *HOLY IS HE* (CHRIST *JESUS*)-
HOLY IS THE GREAT ONE (CHRIST *JESUS*) WHO *DIED FOR ME*.
MARCH 7, 2019

INVALUABLE AND HOLY IS CHRIST JESUS, THE SACRIFICIAL LAMB OF GOD'S DIVINE LOVE AND MERCY

BARBARA SPEAKING

HOLY AND INVALUABLE IS HE (CHRIST *JESUS, THE SACRIFICIAL LAMB OF GOD, THE FATHER*)-
WHO HAS SACRIFICED HIS HOLY PHYSICAL BODY FOR *YOU AND ME*.
HOLY AND PRICELESS IS *GOD ALMIGHTY*-
FOR HE CANNOT BE COMPARED TO, OR WORTH ANY RANGE AND AMOUNT OF GOLD OR *MANMADE MONEY*.
HE IS PRICELESS AND *INVALUABLE TO US,*
FOR HE IS THE SACRIFICIAL LAMB, KNOWN TO US AS *CHRIST JESUS.*
HOLY IS *HIS VALUABLE NAME*-
ETERNITY IS *HIS REALM OF VALUE AND FAME*.
HOLY, HOLY, HOLY ONE!
ALL PRAISES GO OUT TO CHRIST *JESUS,* *THE PRICELESS AND INVALUABLE ONLY BEGOTTEN SON*.
MARCH 6, 2019

THERE IS NO END TO YOUR HOLY LOVE AND MERCY, O PRECIOUS BLOOD OF THE LAMB OF GOD

BARBARA SPEAKING TO CHRIST JESUS' PRECIOUS LIFE REWARDING BLOOD

THERE IS NO END TO YOUR MERCY, **O PRECIOUS BLOOD THAT FLOWS-**
THERE IS NO END TO YOUR EXPRESSION OF LOVE THAT **NO ONE KNOWS.**
FOR YOU, O PRECIOUS BLOOD OF **CHRIST JESUS, THE SACRIFICIAL LAMB OF GODLY LOVE-**
CONTINUOUSLY SEND OUT YOUR HEAVEN BOUND INVITATION TO THE ENTRANCE OF **SWEET HEAVEN ABOVE.**
FOR HOLY AND **FLOWING ARE YOU,**
O PRECIOUS BLOOD THAT FLOWS FROM THE BODY OF HE *(THE CRUCIFIED LORD JESUS)* WHO IS **VICTORIOUS, LONG SUFFERING AND TRUE.**
O PRECIOUS **BLOOD OF MERCY-**
I PRAISE YOU FOR SHARING WITH OUR LOVED ONES, **YOUR KINGDOM OF GLORY.**
MERCY, MERCY, **DIVINE MERCY-**
FLOWS FROM THE WOUNDS THAT RELEASE THE PRECIOUS BLOOD OF **CHRIST, THE ALMIGHTY.**
MARCH 7, 2019

WILL YOU DRINK FROM MY CUP OF DIVINE LOVE, SAYS CHRIST JESUS, THE SACRIFICIAL LAMB?

CHRIST JESUS, THE SACRIFICIAL LAMB, SPEAKING TO THE BELIEVING ONES

WILL YOU DRINK FROM **MY CUP OF LOVE-**
THAT IS FILLED WITH **MY SACRED BLOOD?**
WILL YOU DRINK FROM **MY CUP OF LIFE, DEAR ONES?**
WILL YOU DRINK THE BLOOD THAT WAS SHED FOR **THE SACRIFICIAL LAMB'S WORTHY DAUGHTERS AND SONS?**
WILL YOU, **O BLESSED ONE-**
DRINK THE BLOOD OF LIFE THAT WAS SHED FOR THE CHILDREN OF **GOD, THE FATHER'S, WORTHY SON** *(CHRIST JESUS)*?
FOR, **MY CUP OF LOVE-**
DESCENDED TO YOU FROM **HEAVEN ABOVE.**

HOLY IS THE BLOOD-
OF *CHRIST JESUS,* THE ORIGIN OF ***DIVINE MERCY AND LOVE.***
MARCH 8, 2019

THE AMAZING *BLOOD OF CHRIST* JESUS

BARBARA SPEAKING

FLOW! FLOW! ***FLOW, O AMAZING BLOOD!***
FLOW FROM THE MANY PRECIOUS WOUNDS OF OUR ***HOLY GOD OF LOVE.***
FLOW OVER US-
FLOW, O AMAZING ***BLOOD OF CHRIST JESUS!***
OH HOW AMAZING-
YES, THE LOVE AND BLOOD OF *CHRIST JESUS,* ***THE GREAT AND HOLY KING!***
OH HOW ***AMAZING AND GREAT-***
IS THE BLOOD THAT FLOW OVER THE PEOPLE AND THINGS THAT THE ***HOLY KING*** (*CHRIST JESUS*) ***AND GOD, THE FATHER, CREATE.***
MARCH 8, 2019

THE REIGNING *BLOOD OF CHRIST* JESUS

BARBARA SPEAKING

VICTORY! VICTORY-
IS IN THE PRECIOUS BLOOD OF OUR ***EVERLASTING KING, CHRIST ALMIGHTY.***
FOR ***HOLY IS THE BLOOD-***
THAT REIGNS ON EARTH WITH THE POWER AND PRESENCE OF ***GOD ALMIGHTY'S CONTINUOUS LOVE.***
HOLY IS THE BLOOD-
THAT REIGNS IN THE MIDST OF ***CHRIST JESUS' CHILDREN OF LOVE.***
FOR ***HIS HOLY BLOOD-***
REIGNS ON EARTH, AND IN ***SWEET HEAVEN ABOVE.***
IT IS THE PRECIOUS BLOOD OF ***THE LAMB OF ALMIGHTY GOD-***
THAT REIGNS WITH THE POWER OF ***CHRIST JESUS' DIVINE MERCY AND LOVE.***
MARCH 8, 2019
.

THE BLOOD OF VICTORY AND GODLY FAME

BARBARA SPEAKING

THE BLOOD OF VICTORY-
HAS SAVED THE BELIEVING CHILDREN OF CHRIST ALMIGHTY.
CHRIST'S BLOOD OF VICTORY-
REIGNS AND RULES IN THE MIDST OF HIS GLORY.
FOR, VICTORIOUS AND HOLY-
IS THE SACRIFICIAL BLOOD OF GOD ALMIGHTY.
HOLY, HOLY, HOLY-
IS THE PRECIOUS LIVING BLOOD OF VICTORY!
HOLY IS THE BLOOD-
THAT DESCENDED FROM HEAVEN WITHIN THE PHYSICAL BODY OF CHRIST JESUS, OUR HEAVEN SENT GOD. MARCH 8, 2019

THE LIVING BLOOD OF CHRIST JESUS

BARBARA SPEAKING

THE LIVING BLOOD OF CHRIST JESUS-
SAVES THE CHOSEN ONES, AS IT SURROUNDS BELIEVING AND FAITHFUL US.
THE LIVING BLOOD-
SHINES WITH THE BRILLIANCE OF CHRIST JESUS' GLORY AND DIVINE LOVE.
HOLY IS THE LIVING BLOOD-
THAT REVEALS GOD, OUR BLESSED FATHER'S, REALM OF HEAVENLY MERCY AND LOVE.
MY BLESSED SPIRIT WILL DWELL WITHIN JESUS' LIVING BLOOD OF LOVE,
AS THE BELIEVING ONES FOLLOW HE (CHRIST JESUS) WHO DESCENDED FROM THE OPEN GATES OF HEAVEN ABOVE.
FLOW, FLOW, FLOW, O PRECIOUS LIVING BLOOD OF CHRIST JESUS.
FLOW OVER YOUR BELIEVING ONES AS WE GIVE PRAISE TO HE (CHRIST JESUS).
WHO SAVES WORTHY AND BLESSED US.
MARCH 8, 2019

THE LIVING PRECIOUS BLOOD OF CHRIST JESUS WATCHES OVER AND PROTECTS ME

BARBARA SPEAKING

THE PRECIOUS BLOOD OF CHRIST JESUS-
WATCHES OVER AND PROTECTS US.
THE PRECIOUS BLOOD-
WATCHES OVER AND PROTECTS ME WITH ITS REALM OF SACRED LOVE.
HOLY IS CHRIST JESUS' PRECIOUS BLOOD-
HOLY IS THE BLOOD THAT WATCHES OVER ME IN THE MIDST OF SATAN'S UNHOLY DESTRUCTION AND LOVE.
HOLY IS THE PRECIOUS BLOOD OF THE LAMB OF GOD ALMIGHTY.
ETERNAL IS THE GIFT OF LIFE THAT CHRIST JESUS' HOLY BLOOD GIVES TO THE WORTHY.
MARCH 8, 2019

CAPTURED AND SAVED BY THE PRECIOUS BLOOD OF CHRIST JESUS

BARBARA SPEAKING TO THE PRECIOUS BLOOD OF CHRIST JESUS

CAPTURE ME! CAPTURE ME,
O PRECIOUS BLOOD OF CHRIST ALMIGHTY!
SAVE AND BLESS ME, O HOLY ONE.
SAVE AND BLESS THE FATHER'S (JEHOVAH) DAUGHTER (BARBARA) OF GOD, THE FATHER'S, ONLY BEGOTTEN SON (CHRIST JESUS)!
SAVE ME, CHRIST JESUS, IN THE PRESENCE OF SATAN, THE UNHOLY ONE.
SAVE AND CAPTURE ME, O FLOWING BLOOD OF ALMIGHTY GOD, THE SACRIFICIAL LAMB AND SON!
FOR HOLY AND EVER-FLOWING IS THE BLOOD-
OF THE MIGHTY KING (CHRIST JESUS) OF LOVE.
MARCH 8, 2019

THE SANCTITY OF THE SACRIFICIAL LAMB'S BLOOD HAS CLEANSED THE BELIEVING ONES, SAYS THE LORD GOD

THE LORD GOD SPEAKING

THE SANCTITY OF MY LIVING BLOOD HAS CLEANSED THOSE WHO DESIRE TO *FOLLOW ME*-
FOR IT IS THE HOLY LIFE SAVING FOOD THAT *LEADS BLESSED THEE.*
MY HOLY BLOOD PURIFIES *THE BELIEVING ONES,*
FOR I GIVE LIFE TO THOSE WHO ARE MY LIVING WITNESSES AND *MY OBEDIENT DAUGHTERS AND SONS.*
HOLY ARE THEY-
WHO ARE CLEANSED WITH THE HOLY BLOOD THAT *LEADS TO MY LIFE REWARDING WAY.*
FOR *MY LIVING BLOOD*-
SANCTIFIES THOSE *WHOM I LOVE.*
YOU HAVE BEEN RESTORED AND CLEANSED BY THE POWER OF MY SANCTIFIED BLOOD, *MY CHILDREN.*
YOU HAVE BEEN PURIFIED BY HE WHO LOVES *HIS GREATEST CREATION* (HUMAN BEINGS).

MARCH 9, 2019

GLORIOUS AND MARVELOUS, THE BLOOD OF CHRIST JESUS, THE SACRIFICIAL LAMB OF GOD, THE DIVINE FATHER

BARBARA SPEAKING

OH, THE GLORY-
OH, THE *DIVINE BEAUTY*-
THAT SHINES AND GLOWS FROM THE PRECIOUS BLOOD OF *REIGNING CHRIST ALMIGHTY!*
OH, THE *MAGNIFICENCE AND JOY*-
OF THE HOLY BLOOD THAT CLEANSES EVERY *REPENTANT GIRL AND BOY.*
HOLY IS THE ONE (JEHOVAH GOD, THE FATHER)-
WHO GAVE US THE *SACRIFICIAL LAMB AND SON.*
HOLY AND *ETERNAL IS HE* (CHRIST JESUS)

WHO WAS MADE A DIVINE SACRIFICE FOR *YOU AND ME.*
GLORY, GLORY, GLORY-
SURROUNDS THE BLOOD THAT FLOWED FROM THE WOUNDS OF *SACRIFICIAL GOD ALMIGHTY.*
HOLY IS HE (CHRIST *JESUS*)-
WHO WAS SLAIN ON *SWEET CALVARY.*
HOLY AND *RIGHTEOUS IS HE* (CHRIST *JESUS*)-
WHO MADE A GREAT SACRIFICE FOR *YOU AND ME.*
OH, HOW MARVELOUS THE *BLOOD OF GOD'S CHOSEN ONE* .
LIFE SAVING AND GRACIOUS IS THE *FATHER'S SACRIFICED HOLY SON* .
GLORY, GLORY, *GLORY HALLELUJAH-*
TO THE MIGHTY SACRIFICIAL SON OF *ALMIGHTY GOD, THE FATHER, JEHOVAH!!!*
MARCH 9, 2019

WRAPPED WITHIN THE SACRED BLOOD THAT *REDEEMS THE REPENTANT ONES*

BARBARA SPEAKING

WRAPPED WITHIN-
THE PRECIOUS BLOOD THAT WAS SHED FOR ME, THAT FLOWED FROM THE WOUNDS OF *CHRIST JESUS,* MY *HOLY SACRIFICIAL GOD AND FRIEND.*
WRAPPED WITHIN THE BLOOD-
THAT REVEALS OUR VICTORIOUS SAVIOR'S *UNCONDITIONAL MERCY AND DIVINE LOVE.*
MARCH 9, 2019

THE AMAZING GIFT THAT *DESCENDED FROM HEAVEN TO ME*

BARBARA SPEAKING

THE AMAZING *GIFT OF GOD'S LOVE-*
DESCENDED TO ME IN THE FORM OF *CHRIST JESUS' LIFE SAVING SACRED BLOOD.*
THE GIFT OF *HEAVENLY GOLD* (CHRIST *JESUS'* LIFE SAVING SACRED BLOOD)-
COVERS *GOD'S WORTHY FOLD.*
OH HOW GREAT, *THE BLOOD OF CHRIST JESUS-*
YES, THE AMAZING GIFT THAT *DESCENDED TO BLESSED US!*

HOLY, HOLY, HOLY-
IS THE AMAZING LIFE SAVING BLOOD OF **CHRIST ALMIGHTY!!!**
MARCH 9, 2019

I THANK YOU, LORD **JESUS**, FOR THE PRECIOUS LIFE SAVING BLOOD THAT YOU SHED FOR US, *THE BELIEVING ONES*

BARBARA SPEAKING TO THE LORD **JESUS**, THE SACRIFICIAL LAMB OF ALMIGHTY GOD, THE FATHER

I THANK YOU FOR YOUR PRICELESS PRECIOUS BLOOD THAT YOU SHED, **LORD JESUS.**
I THANK YOU FOR LOVING AND **CARING FOR ALL OF US.**
FOR HOLY IS **YOUR PRECIOUS BLOOD**-
THAT FLOWS OVER THE BODIES AND SOULS OF **YOUR CHILDREN OF LOVE.**
THE BLOOD THAT **YOU SHED**-
WAKENS THE SPIRITS OF THE **WORTHY AND THE DEAD.**
HOLY IS THE BLOOD THAT WAS **SHED FOR US,**
FOR IT GIVES LIFE EVERLASTING TO THE BELIEVING **CHILDREN OF CHRIST JESUS.**
HOLY IS THE **LIFE SAVING BLOOD TODAY**-
FOR IT LEADS US TO **JESUS' HOLY REWARDING WAY.**
MARCH 9, 2019

O HOLY BLOOD THAT **DESCENDS TO ME EVERY DAY**

BARBARA SPEAKING TO THE HOLY BLOOD OF CHRIST **JESUS**

O HOLY BLOOD THAT **DESCENDS TO ME DAILY**-
AS I BOW IN THE PRESENCE OF THE SACRIFICIAL LAMB, **CHRIST, THE ALMIGHTY.**
FOR HOLY IS **JESUS' BLOOD OF LOVE**-
THAT DESCENDS TO MY REALM OF PEACE, FROM **SWEET HEAVEN ABOVE.**
HOLY IS THE HEAVEN DESCENDED **BLOOD OF LOVE**-
THAT DESCENDS FROM THE SACRIFICIAL LAMB WHO **REIGNS IN SWEET HEAVEN ABOVE.**
HOLY, HOLY, HOLY-

IS THE DESCENDED BLOOD THAT WAS SHED FOR US, BY **CHRIST ALMIGHTY!**
FOR WITHIN CHRIST *JESUS'* **BLOOD OF PEACE-**
OUR FEARS AND DOUBTS ARE **BANISHED AND RELEASED.**
O HOLY AND RIGHTEOUS BLOOD THAT **DESCENDS TO ME EVERY DAY-**
CLING TO MY BLESSED SPIRIT AND SOUL, AS I FOLLOW **YOUR LIFE SAVING WAY.**
MARCH 9, 2019

MY HOLY BLOOD: MY EVER-FLOWING FOUNTAIN OF YOUTH, *SAYS CHRIST JESUS, THE SACRIFICIAL LAMB OF ALMIGHTY GOD, THE FATHER*

CHRIST *JESUS*, THE SACRIFICIAL LAMB OF ALMIGHTY GOD, THE FATHER, SPEAKING

MY EVER-FLOWING **FOUNTAIN OF YOUTH** (CHRIST *JESUS'* BLOOD)-
REVEALS TO YOU, **MY HEAVEN SENT TRUTH.**
FOR, **HOLY IS MY FOUNTAIN** (CHRIST *JESUS'* BLOOD)-
THAT FLOWS OVER EVERY **BELIEVING WOMAN AND MAN.**
HOLY IS THE BLOOD-
THAT FLOWS OVER **THOSE WHOM I LOVE.**
FOR, MY FLOWING **FOUNTAIN OF YOUTH** (CHRIST *JESUS'* BLOOD)-
MAKES WAY FOR **MY REALM OF TRUTH.**
FLOW! FLOW! FLOW!
FLOW, O PRECIOUS BLOOD OF MINE, WHEREVER **MY BELIEVING LITTLES GO.**
FOR THEY DESIRE TO **SEE AND FEEL-**
THE SALVATION THROUGH ME, THAT IS **HOLY AND REAL.**
O BLESSED FOUNTAIN OF YOUTH: FLOW OVER **MY LOVED ONES TODAY.**
FLOW OVER THOSE WHO DESIRE **MY LIFE SAVING HOLY WAY.**
HOLY IS **THE FOUNTAIN OF TRUTH** (CHRIST *JESUS'* BLOOD)-
THAT FLOWED OVER MY CHOSEN ONES SINCE THEIR **PHYSICAL AND SPIRITUAL BIRTH.**
FOR **HOLY ARE THEY-**
WHO RECEIVE **MY FOUNTAIN OF YOUTH TODAY.**
MARCH 15, 2019

SWEET CALVARY: *THE BATTLE GROUND OF VICTORY AND EVERLASTING FAME*

BARBARA SPEAKING

SWEET CALVARY, SWEET CALVARY-
IS WHERE THE *BLOOD OF LIFE WAS SHED FOR BLESSED YOU AND ME.*
FOR *HOLY AND REAL-*
IS THE BATTLE THAT WE CAN *SEE AND FEEL!*
HOLY AND TRUE-
IS THE BATTLE ON SWEET CALVARY BETWEEN *CHRIST, THE SACRIFICIAL LAMB OF GOD, ME AND YOU.*
HOLY, HOLY, HOLY-
IS THE BATTLE THAT *SAVED YOU AND ME!*
FOR THE *SACRIFICIAL ACT OF CHRIST JESUS-*
WON THE BATTLE OVER THE SIN THAT *CAPTURES BLESSED US.*
FOR *HOLY AND REAL-*
IS SWEET CALVARY, *THE GOD ASSIGNED BATTLEFIELD!*
HOLY AND REAL-
IS THE BATTLE THAT SATAN DID NOT, AND *CANNOT STEAL!*
MARCH 24, 2019

THE SINS THAT *LEFT THIS DOOMED WORLD*

BARBARA SPEAKING

LOOK AT THEM GO!
LOOK, EVERYONE, AS THE *SINS NO LONGER SHOW.*
FOR *CHRIST JESUS,* THE PRECIOUS *LAMB OF GOD-*
REMOVED THE SINS THAT CAPTURED THOSE WHOM *HE AND FATHER LOVE.*
BY HIS SACRIFICIAL DEATH ON *THE HOLY CROSS-*
HE REMOVED THE SINS OF THE *REPENTANT LOST.*
FOR *HOLY IS HE* (CHRIST *JESUS*)-
WHO HAS REMOVED THE SINS OF *REPENTANT ME.*
FOR *CHRIST JESUS' SACRIFICIAL LOVE-*
HAS WASHED AWAY MY SINS, WITH THE POWER OF *HIS FLOWING LIFE SAVING BLOOD.*

HOLY AND ***TRUE IS HE*** (CHRIST *JESUS*)-
WHO REMOVED THE SINS THAT ***CAPTURED REPENTANT YOU AND ME.***
OH WHAT ***A DIVINE DELIGHT-***
FOR MY SINS ARE NO LONGER WITHIN ***MY HOLY GOD'S SIGHT!***
FOR ***RIGHTEOUS AND REAL-***
IS THE LOVE THAT GOD, THE FATHER, AND GOD, THE SON, FOR THE REPENTANT ONES, ***DO FEEL.***
HOLY AND TRUE-
IS THE SACRIFICED BLOOD THAT WAS ***SHED FOR ME AND YOU.***
REJOICE! REJOICE! REJOICE!
LET ALMIGHTY GOD, HOLY ONE, HEAR ***YOUR REPENTANT UNIFIED VOICE!***
FOR ***HOLY, YOU SEE-***
IS THE PRECIOUS LIFE SAVING BLOOD THAT WAS GIVEN, TO ***REMOVE THE SINS THAT PLAGUED YOU AND ME.***
HOLY IS THE BLOOD-
THAT EXHIBITS ***DIVINE SENT LOVE.***

MARCH 24, 2019

AND ALL WILL WITNESS THE POWER OF THE SACRIFICIAL LAMB OF GOD'S LIFE SAVING BLOOD, *SAYS CHRIST JESUS, THE SACRIFICED ONE*

SOON AND VERY SOON, ALL WILL WITNESS THE POWER AND MAGNIFICENCE OF CHRIST JESUS AND HIS PRECIOUS FLOWING BLOOD

BARBARA SPEAKING

SOON, AND VERY SOON, *EVERYONE WILL WITNESS AND SEE-*
THE HOLY POWER AND PRESENCE OF THE PRECIOUS LIFE SAVING BLOOD THAT WAS *SHED FOR YOU AND ME.*
SOON AND VERY SOON, *ALL WILL SEE-*
THE EVER-FLOWING BLOOD THAT COMES FROM THE LOVE AND MERCY OF *CHRIST, THE ALMIGHTY.*
SOON AND VERY SOON, *ALL WILL BEHOLD-*
THE PRECIOUS BLOOD THAT WAS SHED FOR *GOD'S WORTHY FOLD.*
FOR *HOLY AND TRUE-*
IS THE PRECIOUS BLOOD THAT WAS *SHED FOR ME AND YOU.*
SOON, SOON, SOON, WE WILL *ALL WITNESS-*
THE GLORY THAT SHINES FROM THE REALM THAT RELEASES *THE SACRED BLOOD AND ITS GOODNESS.*
FOR *HOLY IS THE BLOOD-*
THAT REVEALS THAT SACRED ONE'S *(CHRIST JESUS) SACRIFICIAL MERCY AND LOVE.*
MARCH 16, 2019

SPEAK OF MY PRECIOUS LIFE SAVING BLOOD AND ME, MY DAUGHTER (*BARBARA*), SAYS CHRIST JESUS, THE SACRIFICIAL LAMB OF ALMIGHTY GOD, THE FATHER

CHRIST JESUS, THE SACRIFICIAL LAMB OF ALMIGHTY GOD, THE FATHER, SPEAKING TO BARBARA

SPEAK OF MY EVER-FLOWING BLOOD AND ME, *MY WORTHY DAUGHTER (BARBARA).*
SPEAK OF THE EVERLASTING GIFT *(THE PRECIOUS BLOOD OF CHRIST JESUS)* THAT WAS GIVEN BY *GOD, OUR HOLY HEAVENLY FATHER.*
SPEAK OF *MY PRECIOUS BLOOD-*
THAT DESCENDS TO THOSE WHOM *THE FATHER AND I LOVE.*
SPEAK OF MY HOLY LIFE SAVING *REWARD AND WAY.*

SPEAK, DEAR DAUGHTER OF MINE, OF **MY HOLY PRESENCE TODAY.**
FOR **HOLY AND TRUE-**
IS THE BLOOD THAT WAS **SHED FOR ALL OF YOU.**
ETERNAL AND EVERLASTING-
IS THE BLOOD OF **CHRIST, THE LIVING KING.**
SPEAK, DEAR DAUGHTER-
SPEAK TO EVERYONE WHOM I SEND YOU TO, ABOUT THE LIVING BLOOD THAT WAS SHED BY **CHRIST, YOUR GOD AND FATHER.**
SPEAK TO THEM **TODAY,**
SO THAT THEY MAY LEARN OF THE **ONLY ETERNAL LIFE SAVING HOLY WAY.**
SPEAK TO THE **NON-BELIEVING ONES-**
SPEAK TO SATAN'S **CAPTIVE DAUGHTERS AND SONS.**
FOR I, THE SACRIFICIAL LAMB, **DESIRE THAT YOU-**
REVEAL THE PRESENCE OF HE (CHRIST JESUS) WHO IS **HOLY, ETERNAL, LIFE SAVING AND TRUE.**
MARCH 16, 2019

THE LOVE OF CHRIST JESUS' PRECIOUS BLOOD CALLS THOSE WHO HAVE AVOIDED HIM THROUGH THE YEARS.

CHRIST JESUS SPEAKING TO THE LOST ONES

I HAVE SENT OUT **MY INVITATION TO YOU AGAIN,**
SO THAT YOUR ETERNAL SOULS WILL NOT BE CAUGHT UP IN **HELL'S SPIRITUAL UNENDING FIERY RAIN.**
I AM CALLING YOU, **YOU SEE,**
FOR I AM DIVINE COMPASSION AND **EVERLASTING MERCY.**
I AM CALLING **MY LITTLE ONES.**
I AM CALLING **MY LOST DAUGHTERS AND SONS.**
FOR **HOLY AND TRUE-**
IS THE VOICE THAT **CALLS BLESSED YOU.**
LISTEN! LISTEN! LISTEN!
LISTEN TO MY HOLY CALL, O **BLESSED AND LOST CHILDREN.**
FOR **HOLY AND TRUE-**
IS THE COMPASSIONATE **BLOOD THAT SUMMONS YOU.**
COME! COME! COME!

ENTERED, O CALLED ONES, *MY EARTHLY KINGDOM.*
FOR *HOLY AND TRUE-*
IS THE LIFE SAVING *GOD WHO SUMMONS YOU.*
I AM CALLING YOU TODAY-
COME, O LOST SOULS, AND FOLLOW *MY LIFE SAVING ONLY WAY.*
I AM THE ONLY WAY TO *LIFE AND FREEDOM.*
I AM HE WHO RULES *THIS EARTHLY KINGDOM.*
COME! COME! *COME, O BLESSED ONES!*
ENTER MY REALM OF TRUTH, O *CALLED DAUGHTERS AND SONS.*
MARCH 20, 2019

MY MERCY AND LIFE SAVING BLOOD *WILL NEVER LEAVE THE CHOSEN ONES,* *SAYS THE LORD GOD*

CHRIST *JESUS,* THE LORD GOD, SPEAKING

MY HOLY BLOOD WILL *NEVER LEAVE-*
THE SOULS WHOM *I DESIRE TO RETRIEVE.*
FOR *HOLY AND TRUE-*
ARE THE PRECIOUS VOICE AND BLOOD THAT *CALLS YOU.*
HOLY, YOU SEE-
IS THE PRECIOUS BLOOD THAT *CALLS OUT TO BLESSED THEE.*
FOR MY MERCY *ENDURES, DEAR ONE.*
IT ENDURES FOR THE SAKE OF MY BELOVED *DAUGHTER AND SON.*
MARCH 20, 2019

MY SON: MY BLOOD OF LIFE HAS BEEN SENT OUT TO *BLESSED YOU*

CHRIST *JESUS,* SPEAKING TO HIS EARTHLY SONS

MY SON-
O WORTHY AND *CALLED ONE.*
I AM *SENDING OUT TO YOU-*
A GIFT OF LOVE THAT IS *HOLY AND TRUE.*
FOR, *I, THE LORD GOD-*
DESIRE THAT YOU EXPERIENCE AND LEARN OF *MY HOLY LOVE.*

FOR *HOLY AND TRUE-*
IS *JEHOVAH GOD,* WHO *CALLS BLESSED YOU.*
WHAT WILL IT BE, *MY SON?*
WILL YOU HONOR THE CALL OF *ALMIGHTY GOD, THE HOLY ETERNAL ONE?*
MARCH 20, 2019

I EXTEND MY INVITATION OF MERCY TO YOU AGAIN, SAYS CHRIST JESUS' SACRIFICIAL BLOOD

CHRIST *JESUS'* SACRIFICIAL BLOOD OF LIFE SPEAKING

OUT OF DIVINE ME-
I SEND MY INVITATION OF *MERCY TO THEE.*
THROUGH *BARBARA, MY DEVOTED MESSENGER AND BRIDE-*
I SEND OUT AN INVITATION OF A LOVE THAT *I WILL NOT HIDE.*
FOR *HOLY AND TRUE-*
IS THE LIVING BLOOD THAT *CALLS OUT TO YOU.*
HOLY AND TRUE-
IS THE LOVE THAT AGAIN, *CALLS OUT TO BLESSED YOU.*
FOR *MY REALM OF MERCY-*
HAS BEEN *SENT TO THEE.*
WILL YOU HEED *MY HOLY CALL-*
BEFORE SATAN'S REALM OF DESTRUCTION AND DOOM *CAUSE YOU TO STUMBLE AND FALL?*
MARCH 20, 2019

THE PRECIOUS BLOOD THAT CALLS YOU, IS HOLY, ETERNAL AND TRUE

BARBARA SPEAKING

THE PRECIOUS *SACRIFICIAL BLOOD-*
RELEASED THE CALL OF *GOD'S HOLY LOVE.*
FOR *HOLY AND REAL-*
IS THE POWER OF *CHRIST JESUS'* PRICELESS BLOOD THAT *THE BELIEVING ONES KNOW AND FEEL.*
FOR *HOLY AND TRUE-*
IS THE BLESSED BLOOD THAT WAS *SHED ON SWEET CALVARY FOR YOU.*
HOLY, HOLY, HOLY-
IS THE SACRIFICIAL BLOOD OF OUR *BLESSED SAVIOR AND GOD, CHRIST ALMIGHTY.*
MARCH 20, 2019

THE GENEROSITY OF THE BLOOD OF CHRIST JESUS

BARBARA SPEAKING

THE DIVINE GENEROSITY-
OF *CHRIST JESUS, THE ALMIGHTY.*
FOR *HOLY AND TRUE-*
IS THE GENEROSITY OF HE *(CHRIST JESUS)* WHO DIED FOR US ON SWEET CALVARY FOR *ME AND YOU.*
GENEROUS AND HOLY-
IS THE PRECIOUS *BLOOD OF GOD ALMIGHTY.*
FOR *HOLY, EVERLASTING AND TRUE-*
IS THE GENEROUS ONE *(CHRIST JESUS)* WHO *SAVES BELOVED ME AND YOU.*
FOR, HOLY IS *SACRIFICIAL HE (CHRIST JESUS)-*
WHO GIVES GOOD THINGS TO *WORTHY YOU AND ME.*
FOR *HOLY AND TRUE-*
IS THE GENEROUS GOD WHO SENDS DOWN HIS BLESSINGS FROM SWEET HEAVEN TO *ME AND YOU.*
FOR, *I NO LONGER NEED,*
BECAUSE THE SACRIFICED ONE *(CHRIST JESUS), DOES FEED.*

HE FEEDS ME WITH *THE NOURISHMENT-*
THAT COMES WITH KNOWING AND FOLLOWING *HIS SACRED COMMANDMENT,*
FOR *HOLY AND REAL-*
IS THE FOOD AND HEAVEN SENT NOURISHMENT THAT MY MIND AND BODY *RECEIVE AND FEEL.*
MARCH 21, 2019

THE DIVINE LIGHT (CHRIST JESUS) OF THE WORLD HAS PIERCED AND OPENED THE EYES OF THE CHOSEN BLINDED ONES

<u>**BARBARA SPEAKING**</u>

THE LIGHT (CHRIST JESUS)-
BY THE HOLY POWER OF *HIS HEAVENLY MIGHT-*
HAS OPENED THE EYES OF THE *SPIRITUALLY BLINDED ONES.*
HE HAS PIERCED THE SOULS OF *HIS WORTHY DAUGHTERS AND SONS.*
FOR, HOLY IS THE LIGHT OF *THE SACRIFICED LAMB OF GOD-*
WHOSE PRECIOUS BLOOD OPENED THE EYES OF THE BLIND ONES WITH *HIS HEAVENLY LOVE.*
FOR *HOLY AND REAL-*
ARE THE HEAVENLY GIFTS THAT *SATAN CANNOT STEAL.*
HOLY AND TRUE-
IS THE BLOOD OF LIGHT THAT GIVES SIGHT TO *GOD'S BLESSED CHOSEN FEW.*
HOLY AND TRUE-
IS THE BLOOD THAT *PIERCES YOU.*
FOR THE *DIVINE LIGHT OF LOVE (CHRIST JESUS)-*
HAS DESCENDED FROM *HEAVEN'S OPEN GATES ABOVE.*
MARCH 21, 2019

BARBARA AND THE SACRED LIVING BLOOD OF *CHRIST JESUS*

THE HOLY GATES TO ETERNAL LIFE HAVE OPENED WIDE FOR *THE RECEIVERS OF CHRIST JESUS' SACRED LIVING BLOOD*

BARBARA SPEAKING

THE HOLY GATES HAVE *OPENED WIDE-*
FOR THOSE WHO DID NOT *TRY TO HIDE.*
THE GATES THAT LEAD TO *SWEET HEAVEN ABOVE-*
HAVE OPENED FOR THOSE WHO TASTED *JESUS' CUP OF FLOWING BLOOD AND DIVINE LOVE.*
FOR *HOLY ARE THE GATES-*
THAT ARE OPEN FOR THE TRIUMPHANT SOUL WHO *NO LONGER WAITS.*
THE GATES HAVE *OPENED WIDE,*
FOR THE BLESSED CHILDREN OF *ALMIGHTY GOD.*

FOR HOLY ARE *GOD'S GATES ABOVE*-
THAT OPEN TO THOSE WHOM *HE DOES TREASURE AND LOVE.*
THE GATES THAT LEAD TO SPIRITUAL *LIFE AND FREEDOM*-
HAVE OPENED FOR THOSE WHO ARE DESTINED TO LIVE IN *GOD'S HEAVENLY KINGDOM.*
FOR HOLY ARE THE GATES THAT *LEAD TO ETERNAL LOVE.*
HOLY ARE THE GATES OF *SWEET HEAVEN ABOVE.*
LET THE RECEIVERS OF *GOD'S MERCY*-
ENTER THE REALM OF *HIS GLORY.*
FOR *HOLY IS HE (ALMIGHTY GOD)*-
WHOSE OPEN GATES *RECEIVE YOU AND ME!*
MARCH 10, 2019

LET US ENTER THE REALM THAT HOUSES CHRIST JESUS' SACRED BLOOD OF LIFE

BARBARA SPEAKING

COME, MY *BROTHERS AND SISTERS!*
HURRY, O BLESSED *SONS AND DAUGHTERS!*
LET US ENTER *THE HOUSE OF LOVE*-
WHERE DWELLS *CHRIST JESUS' SACRED LIFE SAVING BLOOD!*
LET US *RUN WITH GLADNESS*-
TO THE HOLY PLACE THAT *RELEASES GOD'S GOODNESS (JESUS' LIFE SAVING BLOOD)!*
LET US *RUN WITH GREAT JOY*-
TO THE PLACE THAT RESTORES LIFE TO THE SACRIFICIAL LAMB'S *WORTHY LITTLE GIRL AND BOY!*
HURRY TODAY-

AS WE FOLLOW *CHRIST JESUS' LIFE SAVING HOLY WAY!*
LET US ENTER THE HOLY GATES OF *SWEET HEAVEN*-
AS THE SACRED BLOOD OF *CHRIST JESUS,* DESCENDS TO *HIS FAITHFUL AND OBEDIENT CHILDREN.*
LET US ENTER THE REALM WITH *GLADNESS AND PEACE,*
AS WE DRINK THE SACRED BLOOD THAT THE WOUNDS OF *CHRIST JESUS RELEASE.*

MARCH 10, 2019

THE LIVING BLOOD THAT *SAVES AND RESTORES THE WEEPING ONE*

BARBARA SPEAKING

THE LIVING BLOOD OF *CHRIST ALMIGHTY*-
SAVES AND RESTORES THE *WEEPING LIFELESS BODY.*
THE LIVING BLOOD THAT *DESCENDS TO US*-
LIVES WITHIN THOSE WHO FOLLOW AND TRUST THE *SACRIFICIAL LAMB CALLED CHRIST JESUS.*
FOR HOLY IS *THE LIVING BLOOD*-
THAT FLOWED THROUGH THE VEINS AND WOUNDS OF *ALMIGHTY GOD.*
FOR *HOLY IS HE* (CHRIST *JESUS*)-
WHO HAS SHED MUCH PRECIOUS AND PRICELESS BLOOD FOR *YOU AND ME.*
HOLY ARE *THE WOUNDS OF LOVE*-
THAT RELEASED *CHRIST JESUS' LIVING AND SACRED BLOOD.*

MARCH 10, 2019

THE EVERLASTING *AGREEMENT-COVENANT*

BARBARA SPEAKING THE LORD GOD

MY HOLY LORD GOD AND *FATHER ABOVE*-
PLEASE ACCEPT THE AGREEMENT THAT COMES FROM MY HEART AND *SPIRIT OF LOVE.*
IT IS AN AGREEMENT THAT INCLUDES YOUR HOLY COMMANDMENT, FOR I, *YOUR DAUGHTER OF LOVE*-
AGREES TO SERVE, LOVE AND HONOR *MY HOLY GOD ABOVE.*
FOR MY PROMISE AND *COVENANT WITH YOU*-

REVEALS A LOVE AND BIND THAT ARE *EVERLASTING, HOLY AND TRUE.*
HOLY, HOLY, HOLY-
IS THE EVERLASTING COVENANT BETWEEN *YOU AND BLESSED ME!*
MARCH 10, 2019

I WILL HOLD FAST AND TRUE TO THE AGREEMENT AND PROMISE THAT I MADE IN THE PRESENCE OF CHRIST JESUS, THE SACRIFICIAL LAMB, THE ONLY BEGOTTEN AND LIVING SON OF GOD ALMIGHTY

BARBARA SPEAKING THE LORD GOD

MY LORD GOD: I WILL NOT BREAK OR GO AGAINST *OUR AGREEMENT,*
FOR THROUGH THE MANY YEARS, I HAVE KEPT AND FOLLOWED *YOUR HOLY LIFE SAVING BLOOD AND COMMANDMENT.*
I HAVE FOLLOWED *YOUR COMMANDMENT OF LOVE-*
THAT DESCENDED FROM *YOUR HOLY THRONE ABOVE.*
I HAVE LIVED BY *YOUR HOLY WORDS OF LIFE-*
THAT DESCENDED TO ME, YOUR HEAVEN SENT *OBEDIENT AND CHOSEN WIFE.*
MARCH 10, 2019

AND GOD, THE HOLY WORD, CHRIST JESUS, SPEAKS TO AND THROUGH ME

BARBARA SPEAKING

CHRIST JESUS, GOD, THE HOLY WORD, SPEAKS TO AND *THROUGH ME EVERY DAY,* SO THAT HE MAY LEAD HIS WANDERING FLOCK TO *HIS RIGHTEOUS AND HOLY WAY.*
GOD, THE HOLY *UNCHANGING WORD-*
SPEAKS THROUGH ME, SO THAT *HIS MESSAGES WILL BE HEARD.*
HOLY IS *CHRIST JESUS,* ALMIGHTY *GOD, THE LIVING WORD OF TRUTH.*
I WILL LISTEN TO HE (*CHRIST JESUS, ALMIGHTY GOD)* WHO HAS SPOKEN TO ME *SINCE MY YOUTH.*
FOR *HOLY IS HE* (*CHRIST JESUS)-*
WHO SPEAKS TO AND THROUGH *CHOSEN AND BLESSED ME.*
MARCH 11, 2019

GOD, THE HOLY WORD, DESCENDS TO ME EVERY DAY

BARBARA SPEAKING

GOD, THE HOLY WORD, WHICH IS **CHRIST JESUS**-
SPEAKS LIFE SAVING WORDS THAT **SAVE ALL OF US (THE BELIEVING ONES).**
FOR **HOLY IS HE** (CHRIST *JESUS*)-
WHO SPEAKS HIS GODLY WORDS TO AND **THROUGH BLESSED ME.**
GOD, THE HOLY WORD, HAS **COME TO US**-
HE HAS COME IN THE LIVING BODY AND **FORM OF CHRIST JESUS.**
HOLY IS **GOD, THE LIVING WORD** (CHRIST *JESUS*)-
HOLY IS THE GOD WHOSE SPIRIT, IN THE PAST, **WAS HEARD.**
FOR HE SPEAKS THROUGH THOSE WHOM **HE SENDS**-
HE SPEAKS, DEAR ONES, TO THE BELIEVING ONES WHO ARE **HIS EARTHLY FRIENDS.**
MARCH 11, 2019

HALLOW IS THE BLOOD OF CHRIST JESUS, THE SACRIFICIAL LAMB OF GOD, THE FATHER

BARBARA SPEAKING OF THE BLOOD OF CHRIST *JESUS*

HALLOW IS THE BLOOD OF **THE SACRIFICED ONE** (CHRIST *JESUS*)-
HALLOW IS THE BLOOD OF **CHRIST *JESUS*, THE FATHER'S ONLY BEGOTTEN SON.**

FOR **WORTHY AND HOLY**-
IS THE LIVING BLOOD THAT FLOWED FROM THE **VEINS AND WOUNDS OF CHRIST ALMIGHTY.**
HALLOW BE THY BLOOD, LORD *JESUS*.
HOLY AND GLORIOUS IS THE BLOOD THAT WAS **SHED FOR US.**
I WILL WALK IN THE MIDST OF YOUR HOLY BLOOD, **O SACRED ONE** (CHRIST *JESUS*).
FOR YOU HAVE SACRIFICED MUCH FOR **YOUR WORTHY DAUGHTER AND SON.**
HALLOW BE THE **BLOOD THAT WAS SHED**-
HALLOW BE THE BLOOD THAT WILL FOREVER RAISE THE **SLEEPING ONES AND THE DEAD.**

FOR *HOLY, HOLY, HOLY-*
IS THE *BLOOD OF CHRIST ALMIGHTY!*
MARCH 11, 2019

HOLY, HOLY, HOLY IS *THE BLOOD OF CHRIST ALMIGHTY*

BARBARA SPEAKING OF THE BLOOD OF CHRIST *JESUS*

GLORIOUS, GREAT, AND HOLY-
IS THE LIVING BLOOD OF *CHRIST ALMIGHTY.*
COMES, *O BLESSED ONES!*
RECEIVE THE LIFE SAVING HOLY BLOOD, O WORTHY AND *THIRSTY DAUGHTERS AND SONS!*
RECEIVE THE *BLOOD OF LIFE-*
THAT WAS SHED FOR *JESUS'* FAITHFUL CHILDREN, AND *BARBARA, HIS OBEDIENT WIFE.*
RECEIVE *HIS GIFT OF LOVE-*
THAT IS POURED OUT IN THE FORM OF *HIS SACRED BLOOD.*
FOR *HOLY AND TRUE-*
IS THE BLOOD THAT HAS *REDEEMED ME AND YOU.*
HOLY AND TRUE-
IS THE BLOOD THAT WAS *SHED FOR YOU.*
FOR *GRACE AND MERCY-*
SURROUND THE *PRICELESS BLOOD OF CHRIST ALMIGHTY.*
MARCH 11, 2019

THE SACRED BLOOD OF LOVE: THE SACRED BLOOD OF CHRIST JESUS

BARBARA SPEAKING

SACRED IS THE BLOOD THAT COVERS THE SOULS OF **THE BELIEVING ONES**.
SACRED IS THE BLOOD THAT WAS RELEASED FROM CHRIST JESUS' WOUNDS OF FIRE AND PEACE, FOR **HIS PRECIOUS DAUGHTERS AND SONS**.
SACRED IS THE EVER-FLOWING BLOOD OF CHRIST, THE **SLAUGHTERED LAMB OF GOD, THE HOLY ETERNAL ONE**.
SACRED IS THE BLOOD THAT PROTECTS THE FATHER'S **WOUNDED DAUGHTER AND SON**.
FOR **GREAT AND HOLY**-
IS THE BLOOD THAT FLOWS THROUGH THE DIVINE SPIRIT OF **CHRIST JESUS, THE LIVING, AND THE ALMIGHTY**.

MARCH 11, 2019

THE PRECIOUS BLOOD OF CHRIST JESUS LIFTS MY BODY, SPIRIT AND SOUL EVERY DAY

BARBARA SPEAKING

THE PRECIOUS BLOOD OF **MY HOLY GOD**-
LIFTS MY MIND, BODY AND SOUL, DURING THIS **PERIOD OF GODLY LOVE**.
THE PRECIOUS BLOOD OF THE **SACRIFICIAL LAMB OF GOD TODAY**-
CARRIES MY BODY, SPIRIT AND SOUL TOWARD **CHRIST JESUS' LIFE SAVING HOLY WAY**.
FOR **HOLY**-
IS THE PRICELESS BLOOD OF **CHRIST ALMIGHTY**.
HOLY-
IS THE VALUABLE BLOOD THAT LIFTS MY BLESSED SPIRIT IN **THE PRESENCE OF GOD ALMIGHTY**.
FOR THE KNOWLEDGE OF **CHRIST JESUS' PRECIOUS BLOOD**-
LEADS THE BELIEVING ONES THROUGH **HEAVEN'S OPEN GATES ABOVE**.
FOR **HOLY AND TRUE**-
IS THE PRICELESS BLOOD OF JESUS, THAT WAS **SHED FOR ME AND YOU**.

MARCH 12, 2019

THE PURIFYING BLOOD OF CHRIST JESUS WASHES AWAY THE STAIN OF SIN AND UNRIGHTEOUSNESS

BARBARA SPEAKING

THE PURIFYING **BLOOD OF CHRIST JESUS**-
WASHES AWAY THE SINFUL STAIN THAT **CAPTURES VULNERABLE US.**
JESUS' PURE AND HOLY BLOOD-
FILLS OUR REPENTANT SOULS WITH **HIS PERFECT WELL OF DIVINE LOVE.**
HOLY IS THE PURIFYING **BLOOD OF SACRED HE** (CHRIST JESUS)-
WHO HAS WASHED AND PURIFIED WORTHY AND **BLESSED YOU AND ME.**
THE BLOOD OF CHRIST JESUS, THE SACRIFICIAL LAMB, HAS **REMOVED THE STAIN OF SIN**-
BEFORE THE REPENTANT ONES **FUTURE DAYS BEGIN.**
HOLY IS THE BLOOD OF **THE LAMB OF GOD** (CHRIST JESUS)-
THAT WASHES AWAY THE SIN AND STAIN THAT DESTROYS THE ONES THAT **GOD, THE FATHER, AND HIS SACRIFICED SON** (CHRIST JESUS) **LOVE.**
MARCH 12, 2019

CLEANSE AND PURIFY ME, O GREAT AND HOLY BLOOD OF THE SACRIFICIAL LAMB OF GOD

BARBARA SPEAKING

CLEANSE ME! CLEANSE ME,
O PURIFYING **BLOOD OF CHRIST ALMIGHTY.**
CLEANSE MY BLESSED SOUL **TODAY**-
AS I FOLLOW THE SACRIFICIAL LAMB'S **HOLY ETERNAL WAY.**
CLEANSE ME IN THE HOLY PRESENCE OF **GOD, OUR FATHER,**
AS THE BELIEVING ONES AND ME SING PRAISES AS WE **GATHER.**
HOLY IS THE BLOOD-
THAT COMES FROM CHRIST JESUS' BODY OF **DIVINE MERCY AND LOVE.**
HOLY, HOLY, HOLY-
IS GOD'S REALM OF **EVERLASTING LIFE AND GLORY!**
FOR **BLESSED AND HOLY**-
IS HE WHO HAS **PURIFIED AND CLEANSED ME.**

I SALUTE *YOU, O HOLY ONE!*
I SALUTE *CHRIST JESUS,* GOD, THE FATHER'S, ONLY BEGOTTEN AND *SACRIFICIAL LIFE SAVING SON!*
MARCH 12, 2019

CHRIST JESUS, AND HIS EVER-FLOWING BLOOD OF LIFE

BARBARA SPEAKING TO CHRIST *JESUS*

O HOLY GOD ABOVE-
I PRAISE YOU FOR *YOUR PRESENCE AND LOVE.*
FOR YOU, SO LOVINGLY *REVEAL TO ME-*
THE KNOWLEDGE THAT WILL LEAD TO WHAT I NEED TO KNOW AND DO FOR *BLESSED THEE.*
HOLY, HOLY, HOLY-
IS THE SPIRITUAL VOICE AND PROMPTING OF *GOD ALMIGHTY.*
FOR *YOU, SO LOVINGLY-*
REVEAL TO ME, THE GOOD THINGS THAT WILL SET THE SOULS AND SPIRITS OF *YOUR LOVED ONES FREE.*
HOLY AND TRUE-
ARE SPIRITUAL AND *ALL PRESENT AND ALL POWERFUL YOU.*
FOR YOU REVEAL TO ME *EVERY DAY-*
THE THINGS THAT I NEED TO KNOW OF *YOUR HOLY LIFE SAVING WAY.*
HOLY, ETERNAL AND TRUE-
IS THE ONLY GOD WHO SEES ALL OF *HIS OBEDIENT LOVED ONES THROUGH.*
MARCH 16, 2019

I SIT STILL UNTIL I HEAR THE HOLY VOICE OF CHRIST JESUS, THE VICTORIOUS LIFE SAVING LAMB OF GOD

BARBARA SPEAKING

I CAN HEAR IT! *I CAN HEAR IT!*
I CAN HEAR THE HOLY VOICE OF *THE SACRIFICIAL LAMB'S HOLY SPIRIT!*
FOR HE CALLS OUT TO ME *EVERY DAY,*
AS I LISTEN FOR HIS HOLY VOICE WHEN *I SIT AND PRAY.*

FOR, **HOLY IS HE** (CHRIST JESUS)-
WHO HAS SACRIFICED HIS PRICELESS BLOOD FOR **BLESSED ME.**
HOLY AND TRUE-
IS THE BLOOD THAT CHRIST JESUS, THE SACRIFICIAL LAMB, HAS **SHED FOR ME AND YOU.**
I SIT-
FOR, I LISTEN FOR THE HOLY VOICE AND GOD, WHO WILL **NEVER QUIT.**
FOR HE CONTINUOUSLY FIGHTS THE REALM OF EVIL AND DESTRUCTION FOR **YOU AND ME,**
SO THAT OUR SOULS WILL ENJOY THE GIFT OF **LIVING WITH HIM THROUGHOUT SWEET ETERNITY.**
MARCH 16, 2019

REMEMBERING

BARBARA SPEAKING

REMEMBERING- **REMEMBERING-**
THE PRECIOUS BLOOD OF CHRIST JESUS, GOD, THE FATHER'S, **SACRIFICIAL LAMB, AND OUR TRIUMPHANT LORD AND KING.**
YES, I REMEMBER, THE HOLY POWER OF CHRIST JESUS' **FLOWING BLOOD-**
THAT WAS SHED ON SWEET CALVARY FOR THOSE WHOM **HE TREASURES AND DO LOVE.**
I REMEMBER **EVERY BLESSED DAY-**
THE HOLY BLOOD THAT LEADS TO THE **SAVIOR'S HOLY LIFE SAVING WAY.**
FOR, **HOLY IS HE** (CHRIST JESUS)-
WHO MADE A GREAT **SACRIFICE FOR YOU AND ME.**
REMEMBERING, **REMEMBERING-**
THE HOLY SACRIFICE OF **CHRIST, THE LIVING GOD AND KING.**
FOR, **HOLY IS HE** (CHRIST JESUS)-
WHO FIGHTS SATAN AND HIS DEFEATED REALM OF EVIL FOR **YOU AND ME.**
REMEMBERING, **REMEMBERING-**
THE HOLY POWER AND PRESENCE OF CHRIST JESUS, **MY EVERLASTING GOD AND KING!**
MARCH 16, 2019

I HAVE BEEN MADE FREE AND HOLY BY THE PRECIOUS BLOOD OF THE LAMB OF GOD

BARBARA SPEAKING

I HAVE BEEN MADE FREE-
BY THE PRECIOUS BLOOD OF *SACRIFICIAL CHRIST ALMIGHTY*.
I HAVE BEEN FREED FROM THE REALM OF SIN-
THAT HID *THE LOVE WITHIN*.
AND NOW, *MY BLESSED SPIRIT*-
SHARES THE GOOD NEWS ABOUT THE BLOOD OF THE LAMB OF GOD, SO THAT THE BLESSED ONES *MAY HEAR IT*.
FOR *HOLY AND TRUE*-
IS THE LIFE SAVING BLOOD THAT WAS *SHED FOR REPENTANT ME AND YOU*.
HOLY, YOU SEE-
IS THE BLOOD OF THE LAMB THAT WAS *SHED FOR YOU AND ME*.
MARCH 16, 2019

WHEN THE PRECIOUS BLOOD OF THE LAMB OF GOD ENTERED MY BLESSED SOUL AND HOME

BARBARA SPEAKING

WHEN THE PRECIOUS BLOOD OF THE *LAMB OF GOD ENTERED ME*-
I COULD FEEL THE HOLY PRESENCE AND *POWER OF CHRIST ALMIGHTY*.
WHEN THE SACRIFICIAL LAMB'S PRECIOUS BLOOD *ENTERED MY SOUL AND LIFE*-
I GAVE PRAISE TO THE HOLY GOD WHO CHOSE ME TO BE *HIS FAITHFUL MESSENGER AND BLESSED WIFE*.
FOR HOLY AND *ETERNAL IS HE* (CHRIST JESUS)-
WHO CAME TO *SAVE BLESSED ME*.
WHEN THE PRECIOUS BLOOD OF THE LIVING SACRIFICIAL LAMB CAME TO *MY HUMBLED HOME*-
I FELT A HOLY PRESENCE THAT WOULD *NEVER LEAVE US ALONE*.
WHEN THE PRECIOUS BLOOD OF THE *SLAUGHTERED LAMB OF GOD VISITED US*-
WE FELT THE POWER AND KNOWLEDGE OF LIFE SAVING AND REWARDING *CHRIST JESUS.*

FOR **HOLY IS HE** (CHRIST JESUS)-
WHO VISITS THE HOMES AND SOULS OF THOSE WHO ARE **LOVED AND WORTHY.**
MARCH 16, 2019

MY EVERYTHING: THE PRECIOUS BLOOD OF THE SACRIFICIAL LAMB OF GOD

BARBARA SPEAKING

THE PRECIOUS BLOOD-
OF THE HOLY ONE (CHRIST JESUS) WHOM I WILL ALWAYS AND **FOREVER TREASURE AND LOVE.**
MY EVERYTHING-
YES, THE HOLY BLOOD OF CHRIST JESUS, MY LIVING AND **TRIUMPHANT GOD AND KING.**
MY EVERYTHING-
THE HOLY BLOOD THAT MAKES THE SPIRITS AND SOULS OF THE BELIEVING ONES **DANCE AND SING.**
MY EVERYTHING-
YES, THE PRICELESS HOLY BLOOD THAT WAS SHED ON SWEET CALVARY, BY CHRIST JESUS, **OUR HEAVENLY AND EARTHLY KING.**
HOLY AND **EVER LOVING IS HE** (CHRIST JESUS)-
YES, MY EVERYTHING, CHRIST JESUS, **THE ETERNAL AND ALMIGHTY.**
MARCH 16, 2019

I THANK YOU, O LORD, FOR LEADING ME TO YOUR PRECIOUS BLOOD OF LIFE

BARBARA SPEAKING TO CHRIST JESUS, THE SACRIFICIAL LORD AND GOD

I THANK YOU, O **HOLY LORD GOD ABOVE**-
FOR LEADING ME TO YOUR HOLY FLOWING **LIFE SAVING BLOOD OF LOVE.**
I THANK THEE-
FOR THE SACRIFICIAL LIFE SAVING BLOOD THAT FLOWS FROM **THE WOUNDS OF GOD ALMIGHTY.**
I BLESS YOU-
FOR ALL OF THE HOLY GOOD THINGS THAT YOU **SO LOVINGLY, FOR US, DO.**
I THANK THEE-

I THANK YOU, O SACRIFICIAL GOD, *CHRIST, THE ALMIGHTY!*
I THANK YOU-
I THANK HE *(CHRIST JESUS)* WHO IS *ETERNAL, LOVING AND TRUE.*

BARBARA SPEAKING TO GOD'S EARTHLY CHILDREN OF ALL AGES

FOR *HOLY AND TRUE-*
IS THE BLOOD THAT WAS SHED FOR *BLESSED ME AND YOU.*
MARCH 16, 2019

IF IT HAD NOT BEEN FOR THE PRECIOUS BLOOD OF CHRIST JESUS, THE VICTORIOUS LAMB, GOD AND KING

BARBARA SPEAKING

IF IT HAD NOT BEEN FOR THE PRECIOUS FLOWING *BLOOD OF CHRIST JESUS-*
DOOM AND DESTRUCTION WOULD BE THE EVERLASTING DESTINATION OF *ALL OF US.*
IF CHRIST JESUS-
HAD NOT SACRIFICED *HIS HOLY LIFE FOR US-*
EVERLASTING HELL, WOULD *WAIT FOR US.*
BUT THE PRECIOUS FREELY GIVEN *BLOOD OF THE LAMB OF GOD-*
SHOWED HIS POWER AND COMMITMENT THROUGH *HIS ACT OF SACRIFICIAL LOVE.*
FOR HOLY AND *LIFE SAVING IS HE (CHRIST JESUS)-*
WHO SHED HIS BLOOD FOR US SINNERS ON *SWEET CALVARY.*
HOLY AND TRUE-
IS THE SACRIFICED LAMB WHO DIED FOR *ME AND BLESSED YOU.*
MARCH 16, 2019

THE SWEET TASTE OF THE BLOOD OF CHRIST JESUS, THE SACRIFICIIAL LAMB OF THE ETERNAL GOD AND FATHER OF ALL THAT IS GOOD AND HOLY

BARBARA SPEAKING OF THE BLOOD OF CHRIST JESUS, THE SACRIFICIAL LAMB OF ALMIGHTY GOD, THE FATHER

OH, THE SWEET TASTE OF THE LAMB'S *LIFE SAVING HOLY BLOOD*-
HAS INVITED ME INTO *HIS REALM OF SACRED LOVE*.
THE HOLY BLOOD IS *PURE AND SWEET*;
AND THE LIFE REWARDING TASTE LEADS ME TO THOSE WHOM *THE SACRIFICIAL LAMB WANTS ME TO GREET*.
FOR *HOLY IS THE BLOOD*-
THAT REVEALS *LIFE SAVING LOVE*.
I HAVE TASTED *JESUS' PRECIOUS BLOOD OF LIFE*;
AND NOW, I LIVE MY BLESSED LIFE, AS THE *MASTER'S (CHRIST JESUS) WORTHY AND SACRIFICIAL WIFE*.
FOR, HOLY AND PURE IS *THE TASTE*-
OF THE EVER FLOWING LIFE SAVING BLOOD THAT *THE BELIEVING ONES WILL NEVER WASTE*.
FOR *HOLY AND TRUE*-
IS THE SACRIFICIAL BLOOD THAT WAS *SHED FOR ME AND YOU*.
MARCH 17, 2019

YOUR BLOOD: MY BLOOD: OUR BLOOD: THE SACRIFICIAL BLOOD: CHRIST JESUS' LIFE SAVING BLOOD OF DIVINE LOVE

BARBARA SPEAKING TO CHRIST JESUS, THE SACRIFICIAL LAMB OF GOD ALMIGHTY

MY LORD GOD-
I WILL SHARE *YOUR HOLY LIFE GIVING BLOOD*.
FOR *HOLY AND TRUE*-
IS THE POWERFUL BLOOD THAT CAME FROM *BLESSED ETERNAL YOU*.
IF ONLY THE WORLD *COULD SEE*-
THE MAGNIFICENCE OF *CHRIST ALMIGHTY*.
OH WHAT A PITY-

FOR THOSE WHO DO NOT KNOW THE BLOOD THAT WAS *SHED BY THEE.*
FOR *HOLY, ETERNAL, AND REAL-*
IS THE PRICELESS BLOOD THAT *THE BELIEVING ONES TRULY FEEL.*
YOUR PRECIOUS BLOOD-
SENDS OUT RAYS OF SUNSHINE AND *DIVINELY LOVE.*
FOR *HOLY AND TRUE-*
IS THE INVALUABLE BLOOD THAT CAME FROM *WORTHY YOU.*
FOR THERE IS NO *PRICE ON EARTH-*
THAT EQUATES TO OR EXCEEDS YOUR HOLINESS AND *MONETARY WORTH.*
MARCH 17, 2019

NOTHING BUT *THE PRECIOUS BLOOD OF THE LAMB*

BARBARA SPEAKING

NOTHING: NOTHING: NOTHING-
COULD TAKE THE PLACE OF *CHRIST JESUS, THE SLAUGHTERED AND SACRIFICIAL KING.*
NOTHING BUT *HIS PRECIOUS BLOOD-*
COULD EXPRESS THE DEPTH OF *HIS HOLY TRUTH AND HIS LOVE.*
FOR *HOLY AND ETERNAL IS HE* (CHRIST *JESUS*)-
WHO HAS SHED HIS PRECIOUS LIFE SAVING BLOOD FOR *YOU AND ME.*
NOTHING: NOTHING: NOTHING-
COULD FILL THE CUP OF BLOOD THAT WAS GIVEN FOR US, BY *CHRIST JESUS, OUR HOLY AND EVERLASTING GOD AND KING.*
MARCH 16, 2019

FAITHFUL AND TRUE, IS *THE PRICELESS BLOOD THAT WAS SHED FOR BLESSED ME AND YOU*

BARBARA SPEAKING

FAITHFUL-

WONDERFUL-
Holy and True-

IS THE PRICELESS BLOOD THAT WAS *SHED FOR ME AND YOU.*
FOR THE PRICELESS *BLOOD OF CHRIST JESUS*-
REDEEMED AND BLESSED *BELIEVING US.*
FAITHFUL IS *THE HOLY BLOOD-*
THAT SAVED US BY THE GRACE OF ALMIGHTY *GOD'S MERCY AND DIVINE LOVE.*
BY THE HOLY POWER OF *CHRIST ALMIGHTY-*
HIS PRECIOUS BLOOD HAS REDEEMED EVERY *BLESSED SOUL AND BODY.*
FOR, *HOLY AND FAITHFUL-*
IS THE BLOOD THAT WAS SHED BY THE SACRIFICIAL LAMB; *CHRIST JESUS, THE GREAT AND THE WONDERFUL.*
MARCH 16, 2019

AND I BEHELD THE BEAUTY OF *HIS SACRED BLOOD*

BARBARA SPEAKING

IT. *I BEHELD THE BEAUTY-*
OF THE PRECIOUS LIFE SAVING *BLOOD OF CHRIST ALMIGHTY.*
FOR IT WAS *PLAIN TO SEE-*
THE BEAUTY THAT EMITS FROM THE PRECIOUS SACRED BLOOD OF *CHRIST ALMIGHTY.*
FOR *HOLY AND BEAUTIFUL-*
IS THE BLOOD OF ALMIGHTY *GOD, THE GREAT AND WONDERFUL.*
I COULD TRULY SEE-
THE SACRIFICIAL BLOOD OF *CHRIST JESUS THAT WAS SHED FOR BLESSED AND CHOSEN ME.*
I COULD PLAINLY SEE-

THE PRECIOUS LIFE SAVING BLOOD THAT WAS SHED ON *BLESSED SWEET CALVARY.*
FOR BEAUTIFUL, *GRACIOUS AND HOLY-*
IS THE PRICELESS *BLOOD OF GOD ALMIGHTY.*
YES, I COULD *PLAINLY SEE-*
THE GLORIOUS BLOOD THAT *SURROUNDS BLESSED ME.*
FOR *HOLY AND TRUE-*
IS THE BEAUTIFUL BLOOD THAT WAS *SHED FOR ME AND YOU.*
MARCH 18, 2019

A LIVING WITNESS

BARBARA SPEAKING

I AM A *LIVING WITNESS-*
TO THE DIVINE BLOOD AND *ITS MERCY AND GOODNESS.*
FOR, I WAS *BLESSED TO SEE-*
THE DIVINE POWER AND LOVE OF *GOD ALMIGHTY.*
FOR *HOLY, YOU SEE-*
IS THE POWER OF THE LAMB'S BLOOD THAT WAS *REVEALED TO CHOSEN ME.*
HOLY AND TRUE-
IS THE SACRIFICIAL BLOOD AND BODY THAT WAS *OFFERED FOR ME AND YOU.*
I AM A WITNESS, YOU SEE-
OF THE DEPTH OF THE LOVE THAT CAME WITH *THE SACRIFICIAL ACT OF CHRIST ALMIGHTY.*
FOR *HOLY AND TRUE-*
IS THE BLOOD THAT WAS *SHED FOR ME AND YOU.*
I AM A WITNESS TODAY-
FOR I LISTEN TO WHAT THE SACRIFICIAL LAMB OF *GOD HAS TO SAY.*
FOR *HOLY AND TRUE-*
ARE THE LIFE SAVING THINGS THAT *HIS PRECIOUS BODY AND BLOOD DO.*
MARCH 18, 2019

THE PRECIOUS BLOOD THAT WASHED ME WHITE AS HEAVEN SENT SNOW

BARBARA SPEAKING

CLEANSE ME. CLEANSE ME.
CLEANSE MY BODY AND SOUL, O PRECIOUS BLOOD OF CHRIST ALMIGHTY.
WASH MY SINS AWAY-
CLEANSE ME, O HOLY BLOOD, AS I TRAVEL THROUGHOUT THIS BLESSED GOD SENT DAY.
CLEANSE MY SOUL IN THE MORNING-
CLEANSE ME, O HOLY BLOOD THAT WAS SHED BY CHRIST JESUS, THE EVERLASTING KING.
FOR HOLY AND PURIFYING IS THE PRECIOUS BLOOD OF HE (CHRIST JESUS)-
THAT WASHED THE SOUL OF BLESSED ME.
HOLY, HOLY, HOLY AND TRUE-
IS THE FLOWING BLOOD THAT SAVES ME AND WORTHY YOU.

MARCH 19, 2019

I CAN SEE HIM (SATAN)

BARBARA SPEAKING

I CAN SEE-
The unholy presence of *destructive he (satan)*.

I CAN FEEL-
THE UNHOLY PRESENCE OF SATAN, THE DEVIL, THE EVIL ONE, FOR HE IS REAL!
I CAN SEE SATAN, THE DESTRUCTIVE ONE,
FOR HE COMES IN THE FORM OF HIS CAPTIVE HUMAN DAUGHTER AND SON.
I CAN SEE HIM VERY CLEAR,
FOR HIS UNGODLY PRESENCE IS VERY NEAR.
HE COMES IN THE FORM OF FAMILY AND FRIENDS-
AS HE WREAKS THE HAVOC THAT NEVER ENDS.
UNHOLY AND DESTRUCTIVE IS HE (SATAN)-

WHO TRIES TO DESTROY THOSE WHO FOLLOW *THE SACRED BLOOD OF CHRIST ALMIGHTY.*

MARCH 19, 2019

CHRIST JESUS' PRECIOUS BLOOD *RADIATES WITHIN ME*

BARBARA SPEAKING

THE BLOOD OF *THE PRECIOUS SACRIFICIAL LAMB-*
YES, THE RADIANT BLOOD OF *THE GREAT AND HOLY I AM!*
THE HOLY BLOOD, *YOU SEE-*
RADIATES WITHIN BLESSED AND *CHOSEN HEAVEN SENT ME.*
FOR, *HOLY AND TRUE-*
IS THE RADIANT LIGHT AND BLOOD THAT COVER AND SAVE *BLESSED ME AND YOU.*
HOLY, YOU SEE-
IS THE SACRIFICIAL LAMB'S BLOOD THAT *SHINES WITHIN AND THROUGH ME.*
FOR *CHRIST JESUS' RADIANT BLOOD-*
SENDS OUT *HIS HOLY LIGHT AND LOVE.*
FOR *HOLY IS HE (CHRIST JESUS)-*
WHOSE PRECIOUS LIFE SAVING BLOOD *RADIATES WITHIN SENT ME.*

MARCH 19, 2019

HOLY AND TRUE

BARBARA SPEAKING

HOLY AND TRUE-
IS THE BLOOD OF THE LAMB OF GOD THAT IS SENT TO *HIS CHOSEN FEW.*
HOLY AND TRUE-
IS THE INVALUABLE BLOOD OF *CHRIST JESUS,* THAT HE HAS *OFFERED TO BLESSED YOU.*
HOLY AND TRUE-

IS GOD, THE FATHER'S, *LOVE FOR YOU.*
FOR, *CAN YOU NOT SEE-*
THE PRECIOUS BLOOD THAT IS *ETERNAL AND FREE?*
MARCH 19, 2019

HELL CANNOT BEAT NOR CONQUER *THE LIFE SAVING BLOOD THAT WAS SHED FOR US*

<u>**BARBARA SPEAKING**</u>

HELL CANNOT FIGHT-
THE POWER AND GLORY OF THE BLOOD OF THE SACRIFICIAL *LAMB OF GOD'S, HOLY MIGHT.*
HELL CANNOT *CONQUER OR DEFEAT-*
THOSE WHO FOLLOW IN *CHRIST JESUS' SACRED FEET.*
HELL *CANNOT, YOU SEE-*
DEFEAT THE BLOOD OF *GOD, THE ALMIGHTY.*
FOR *HOLY AND TRUE-*
IS THE PRECIOUS BLOOD OF HE *(CHRIST JESUS)* WHO *FIGHTS DAY AND NIGHT FOR ME AND YOU.*
HOLY, HOLY, HOLY-
IS THE VICTORIOUS BLOOD OF *CHRIST, THE ALMIGHTY!*
MARCH 19, 2019

HE DID NOT FOOL ME- HE IS SATAN, *THE LAMB OF GOD'S EVERLASTING ENEMY*

<u>**BARBARA SPEAKING**</u>

HE, THE LOWLY ONE, *DID NOT CAPTURE ME.*
FOR HE IS SATAN, THE SACRIFICIAL LAMB OF *GOD'S, UNHOLY ENEMY.*
HE DID NOT CAUSE FEAR NOR *DESTROY ME-*
FOR I HAVE BEEN COVERED WITH THE PRECIOUS BLOOD OF *CHRIST ALMIGHTY.*
HOLY IS HE (CHRIST JESUS)-
WHO SAVED ME FROM SATAN, *CHRIST JESUS' DESTRUCTIVE ENEMY.*
FOR HOLY AND TRUE*, YOU SEE-*
IS THE PRECIOUS BLOOD OF THE LAMB THAT *RESCUED ME.*

FOR *I DID FLEE*-
FROM THE REALM OF EVIL AND DECEIT THAT TRIED TO *PURSUE AND CAPTURE VULNERABLE ME.*
FOR *HOLY AND TRUE*-
IS THE PRICELESS BLOOD THAT *RESCUES ME AND YOU.*
HOLY AND ETERNAL IS *THE SACRIFICIAL GOD,*
WHO SAVED US FROM SATAN, OUR ENEMY, BY THE POWER AND PRESENCE OF *HIS LIVING BLOOD.*
HOLY AND TRUE-
IS THE SACRED BLOOD THAT *RESCUED AND SAVED BLESSED ME AND YOU.*
MARCH 19, 2019

THE HOLY PRECIOUUS BLOOD OF *MY LOVE, JESUS, THE CHRIST*

BARBARA SPEAKING

THE PRECIOUS BLOOD-
OF HE (CHRIST *JESUS*) WHOM MY REDEEMED *SOUL AND BODY LOVE.*
THE PRECIOUS BLOOD HAS *SENT WORTHY ME*-
TO THE EARTHLY OFFSPRING OF *CHRIST ALMIGHTY.*
HOLY AND TRUE-
IS HE (CHRIST *JESUS*) WHO *LOVES ME AND YOU.*
FOR MY SOUL *DOES LOVE*-
HE (CHRIST *JESUS*) WHO DESCENDED TO US FROM *SWEET HEAVEN ABOVE.*
FOR THE PRECIOUS BLOOD OF CHRIST *JESUS, MY HEAVEN SENT LOVE*-
CAME TO ME FROM *SWEET HEAVEN ABOVE.*
FOR *HOLY, HOLY, HOLY*-
IS MY LOVE FOR *CHRIST JESUS, THE ALMIGHTY.*
THE PRECIOUS BLOOD OF *CHRIST JESUS, MY TRUE LOVE*-
WASHES THE SOULS OF THOSE WHO ARE BOUND FOR *SWEET PARADISE ABOVE.*
FOR *HOLY, YOU SEE*-
IS THE PRECIOUS LOVE AND *BLOOD OF GOD ALMIGHTY.*
MARCH 21, 2019

THE PRECIOUS BLOOD OF *CHRIST JESUS*, SPEAKS TO AND THROUGH ME, HIS SENT MESSENGER OF DIVINE TRUTH, EVERY DAY

BARBARA SPEAKING

HE, THE SACRIFICIAL LAMB OF GOD, THE FATHER, *SPEAKS THROUGH SENT BLESSED ME.*
THE HOLY BLOOD OF LIFE, SPEAKS THROUGH ME, THE DIVINELY SENT *MESSENGER OF CHRIST ALMIGHTY.*
HIS PRECIOUS BLOOD SPEAKS *HEAVENLY TRUTH THROUGH ME.*
THE HOLY BLOOD SPEAKS TO AND THROUGH OBEDIENT AND FAITHFUL ME, THE SERVANT AND *BRIDE OF CHRIST ALMIGHTY.*
FOR *HOLY IS THE BLOOD-*
THAT COVERS ME WITH THE *GIFT OF HEAVENLY LOVE.*
FOR, *HOLY AND TRUE-*
IS THE BLOOD THAT REVEALS THE *TRUTH TO ME AND YOU.*
GLORY, GLORY, GLORY-
TO THE SACRIFICIAL BLOOD THAT SPEAKS THE TRUTH ABOUT *CHRIST ALMIGHTY!*
FOR *HOLY AND ETERNAL IS HE* (CHRIST *JESUS*)-
WHOSE PRECIOUS LIFE SAVING BLOOD SPEAKS TO AND THROUGH *BLESSED ME.*
MARCH 21, 2019

YOU ARE THE HOLY ONE: THE HOLY BLOOD: *CHRIST JESUS*

BARBARA SPEAKING

MY HOLY GOD-
O HOLY BLOOD THAT DESCENDED FROM *HEAVEN'S GATES OF LOVE.*
HOLY AND TRUE-
IS THE PRICELESS BLOOD THAT *DESCENDED WITHIN BLESSED YOU.*
FOR YOU, MY LORD GOD, ARE *THE HOLY ONE-*
YOU, O LORD *JESUS,* ARE *GOD, THE FATHER'S, ONLY BEGOTTEN SON.*
FOR *HOLY AND TRUE-*
IS THE INVALUABLE BLOOD THAT *DESCENDED WITHIN SACRIFICIAL YOU.*
O HOLY ONE (CHRIST *JESUS*)-
YOUR GREAT WORK HAS *TRULY BEGUN!*
FOR *HOLY AND REAL-*
IS THE PRECIOUS BLOOD OF THE LAMB THAT *I CAN SEE AND FEEL!*

March 21, 2019

Satan, the Deceptive One Has Sent Out His Army of Destruction

Barbara Speaking

Satan, the *deceptive one*-
Has sent out his army of thieves to *the messenger and bride (Barbara)* of *God, the Father's, sacrificial triumphant son. (Christ Jesus)*-
Satan has *sent his army*-
To mislead the daughter *(Barbara)* of *Christ Almighty.*
But he *cannot capture nor deceive*-
The daughter *(Barbara)* and messenger who *does receive.*
For I, the daughter and *spiritual bride of Christ Jesus,*
Receive and follow the sacred blood that *covers and saves us.*
For Satan nor *his doomed army*-
Cannot deceive nor steal the soul of *the messenger and bride (Barbara) of Christ, the Almighty.*

March 21, 2019

I Have No Place Nor Space In My Life For Satan's Sent Soul Destroyers

Barbara Speaking

I have no room-
For Satan's delivers of *destruction and doom.*
I have no space-
For those who deceive others by their *Satan guided hidden face.*
For *Holy is He (Christ Jesus)*-
Who protects *vulnerable me.*
Holy and true-
Is the righteous one *(Christ Jesus)* who *sees me through.*
There is no place in my life *for Satan,*
For he sends out to the vulnerable ones, his *captive woman and man.*
He cannot fool or *deceive me,*

FOR I LIVE BY THE HOLY LIFE SAVING **BLOOD OF CHRIST ALMIGHTY.**

MARCH 21, 2019

HE, SATAN, IS BACK AGAIN. *HE COMES IN THE FORM OF A FAMILIAR WOMAN AND MAN*

BARBARA SPEAKING

HE (SATAN) IS BACK AGAIN-
HE COMES IN THE FORM OF A ***FAMILIAR WOMAN OR MAN** (FAMILY OR FRIEND).*
HE COMES IN A FORM THAT *I CAN SEE,*
FOR HIS UNHOLY AND UNWANTED PRESENCE WAS REVEALED TO ME, BY THE DIVINE POWER AND **BLOOD OF CHRIST ALMIGHTY.**
HE COMES IN A FORM THAT *I CAN HEAR-*
BUT, THE BLOOD OF **CHRIST JESUS *IS ALWAYS WITHIN AND NEAR.***
HE COMES IN A FORM THAT I CAN ***OBSERVE AND TOUCH,***
BUT. HE CANNOT ENTER THE SOUL OF SHE *(BARBARA)* WHOM **CHRIST JESUS *LOVES VERY MUCH.***
I CAN HEAR *THEIR UNHOLY VOICE-*
AS MY BLESSED SOUL SINGS SONGS OF PRAISE TO *CHRIST JESUS,* AS ***MY SAVED SPIRIT DANCE AND REJOICE!***
FOR HOLY IS *THE PRECIOUS BLOOD-*
OF THE SACRIFICIAL GOD WHOM I WILL ***ALWAYS SERVE, HONOR AND LOVE.***

MARCH 21, 2019

THE DIVINE BLOOD OF CHRIST JESUS KNOWS SATAN

BARBARA SPEAKING

THE HOLY **BLOOD OF CHRIST JESUS**-
WARNS **VULNERABLE AND UNSUSPECTING US.**
HE WARNS US OF **SATAN'S UNGODLY PRESENCE,**
AS HE TRIES TO INTERRUPT AND CAUSE CONFUSION IN **OUR PLACES OF RESIDENCE.**
FOR HOLY IS THE **PRECIOUS BLOOD OF HE** (CHRIST JESUS)-
WHO WARNS AND PROTECTS **UNSUSPECTING YOU AND ME.**
HOLY AND TRUE-
IS THE INVALUABLE BLOOD THAT FIGHTS SATAN, FOR THE ETERNAL SOULS OF **ME, AND YOU TOO.**
HOLY AND RIGHTEOUS-
IS THE PRECIOUS BLOOD OF SACRIFICIAL **LIFE SAVING CHRIST JESUS.**
MARCH 21, 2019

I WILL FIGHT SATAN, THE DEFEATED BEAST, WITH THE HOLY POWER AND PRESENCE OF THE TRIUMPHANT BLOOD OF CHRIST JESUS, THE VICTORIOUS LAMB OF THE ONLY LIVING GOD

BARBARA SPEAKING

I WILL **FIGHT AND DEFEAT**-
SATAN, THE **FORETOLD UNGODLY BEAST.**
I WILL DEFEAT HIM WITH **THE HOLY POWER**-
THAT FLOWS FROM THE BLOOD OF CHRIST JESUS, EVERY **BLESSED MINUTE AND HOUR.**
I WILL DEFEAT HIS **LOWLY REALM TODAY**-
AS I DENY THOSE WHO FOLLOW **HIS UNHOLY WORD AND WAY.**
I WILL FIGHT THE UNHOLY BEAST, WITH THE POWER AND DIVINE **STRENGTH OF CHRIST JESUS**-
AS I JOIN THE HOLY BLOOD THAT WAS **SHED FOR US.**
FOR HOLY IS **THE BLOOD OF HE** (CHRIST JESUS)-
WHO FIGHTS AND DEFEATS **SATAN'S UNHOLY REALM WITH ME.**
FOR **UNHOLY AND TRUE**-

IS SATAN, THE FORETOLD BEAST, WHOSE GOAL IS TO **DESTROY ME AND YOU.**
HIS UNHOLY PRESENCE **IS REAL-**
FOR HIS UNGODLY WAYS, **I CAN SEE AND FEEL.**
MARCH 21, 2019

SATAN'S REALM OF DARKNESS COULD NEVER PUT OUT THE RADIANT LIGHT THAT SHINES FROM THE LIVING BLOOD OF CHRIST JESUS

BARBARA SPEAKING

SATAN'S REALM OF **DARKNESS-**
COULD NEVER PUT OUT THE BRILLIANT AND RADIANT LIGHT THAT SHINES FROM **THE LIVING BLOOD OF CHRIST *JESUS.***
FOR HOLY IS THE **RADIANT BLOOD OF HE** (CHRIST *JESUS*)-
THAT SHINES WITHIN AND THROUGH **BLESSED SENT ME.**
FOR, THE HOLY **LIGHT OF CHRIST *JESUS-***
DEFEATS THE REALM OF DARKNESS THAT TRIES TO **SLAY AND CAPTURE US.**
FOR HOLY IS **THE RADIANT BLOOD OF HE** (CHRIST *JESUS*)-
THAT WAS SHED FOR US, BY **GOD, THE SACRIFICIAL CHRIST ALMIGHTY.**
HOLY AND TRUE-
IS THE RADIANT LIGHT THAT **PROTECTS ME AND YOU.**
HOLY IS THE LIGHT-
THAT REVEALS THE SACRIFICIAL LAMB OF **GOD'S HOLY MIGHT.**
MARCH 22, 2019

THE HOLY BLOOD OF THE SLAUGHTERED LAMB OF GOD *HAS ENTERED THE OPEN DOORS (HEARTS) OF THE BELIEVING ONES*

BARBARA SPEAKING

THE HOLY BLOOD-
HAS ENTERED THE OPEN DOORS *(HEARTS)* OF THOSE WHOM THE SLAUGHTERED LAMB OF GOD, THE FATHER, AND **CHRIST *JESUS, HIS ONLY BEGOTTEN SON, TRULY LOVE.***
THE HOLY BLOOD HAS **ENTERED WITH DIVINE GRACE-**
AS THE CRUCIFIED KING LOOKED UPON THE BELIEVING ONE'S **EXCITED FACE.**

FOR *HOLY AND TRUE*-
ARE THE BELIEVING ONES WHO *MADE IT THROUGH*.
FOR, THROUGH *HEAVEN'S OPEN GATE*-
THE BELIEVING ONES *NO LONGER HAVE TO WAIT*.
FOR THEY-
TRULY FOLLOW THE SACRIFICIAL LAMB OF GOD AND *HIS HOLY LIFE SAVING WAY*.
YES, THE HOLY BLOOD HAS *ENTERED TODAY*-
THE OPEN HEARTS OF THOSE WHO FOLLOW *THE LAMB OF GOD'S HOLY WAY*.
FOR *HOLY AND REAL*-
IS THE *LOVE THAT THEY FEEL*.
HOLY AND TRUE-
IS THE PRECIOUS BLOOD THAT *ENTERED THEIR HEARTS TOO*.
MARCH 22, 2019

THE BLOOD OF CHRIST JESUS

BARBARA SPEAKING

JESUS' PRECIOUS BLOOD-
YES, THE MIGHTY BLOOD THAT EXPRESSES *GOD, THE FATHER'S, UNDYING LOVE*.
JESUS' BLOOD HAS COME DOWN TO *EARTH*-
TO DWELL IN THE MIDST AND HEARTS OF THOSE WHOM HE HAS CHOSEN BEFORE
THEIR *SPIRITUAL AND PHYSICAL BIRTH*.
FOR *HOLY IS HIS BLOOD*-
THAT SENDS OUT *BLESSINGS AND DIVINE LOVE*.
HOLY IS THE BLOOD OF *CHRIST JESUS*-
HOLY IS THE BLOOD THAT CAME TO LIVE AND MINGLE WITH *BLESSED US*.
FOR HOLY IS THE *BLOOD OF HE* (CHRIST *JESUS*)-
WHO IS KNOWN BY THE HOLY NAME OF *CHRIST ALMIGHTY*.
MARCH 23, 2019

THE PRECIOUS BLOOD OF CHRIST JESUS, THE SACRIFICIAL LAMB OF ALMIGHTY GOD, THE HOLY ONE, INVITES ALL

BARBARA SPEAKING

THE HOLY BLOOD OF *THE LAMB OF GOD*-
INVITES THOSE WHOM *GOD, THE FATHER, AND CHRIST JESUS, THE SON, DO LOVE.*
JESUS' SACRED BLOOD INVITES ALL-
SO THAT THE LOST ONES WILL *NOT STUMBLE OR FALL.*
FOR *HOLY IS THE BLOOD*-
THAT SENDS OUT THE *INVITATION OF DIVINE LOVE.*
AND, *HOLY AND TRUE*-
IS THE BLOOD OF *CHRIST JESUS* THAT *CLEANSES ALL OF YOU.*
CHRIST'S SACRED BLOOD'S *INVITATION OF LOVE*-
COMES FROM SWEET *REWARDING HEAVEN ABOVE.*
FOR HOLY AND RIGHTEOUS IS *THE INVITATION*-
THAT IS SENT TO THOSE OF *EVERY BLESSED PEOPLE AND NATION.*
MARCH 23, 2019

WITHOUT THE LIVING BLOOD OF CHRIST JESUS, THE SINKING ONES WILL FALL AND DROWN

BARBARA SPEAKING

WITHOUT THE PRECIOUS AND *SACRED BLOOD*-
OF HE WHOM THE *BELIEVING ONES LOVE*-
ONE WILL *SINK AND FALL*-
WITHOUT THE ACCEPTANCE OF *ALMIGHTY GOD'S HOLY LIFE SAVING CALL.*
FOR HOLY IS *GOD'S LIFE SAVING BLOOD*-
THAT IS OFFERED TO THOSE WHOM *HE DOES CHERISH AND LOVE.*
HOLY IS HE (CHRIST JESUS)-
WHO SENDS THE GIFT OF LOVE AND *HIS HOLY POWER TO THEE.*
HOLY AND TRUE-
IS THE PRICELESS BLOOD THAT IS *SENT TO ME AND YOU.*
HOLY, HOLY, HOLY-
IS THE INVITING BLOOD OF *CHRIST ALMIGHTY!*

BARBARA ANN MARY MACK

MARCH 23, 2019

THE BLESSED LIGHT THAT SHINES FROM THE SACRED BLOOD OF THE LAMB OF GOD

BARBARA SPEAKING

MY BROTHERS AND SISTERS: CAN YOU SEE-
THE BRILLIANT SACRED LIGHT THAT COMES FROM THE BLOOD OF CHRIST ALMIGHTY?
CAN YOU SEE, DEAR ONES-
THE HOLY LIGHT OF LOVE THAT PIERCES THE BLESSED EYES AND SOULS OF THE SACRIFICIAL LAMB'S WORTHY DAUGHTERS AND SONS?
OH THE BRILLIANT LIGHT-
PIERCES THE BELIEVING ONES DARKEST AND GLOOMY NIGHT.
FOR HOLY, YOU SEE-
IS THE BRILLIANT LIGHT THAT SHINES FROM THE BLOOD OF CHRIST JESUS, OVER YOU AND ME.

MARCH 23, 2019

I DO NOT WORRY, NOR SHOW CONCERN, BECAUSE THE LIVING BLOOD OF CHRIST JESUS, TAKES VERY GOOD CARE OF MY FAMILY AND ME

BARBARA SPEAKING TO THE SACRED BLOOD AND CHRIST JESUS, THE ALMIGHTY

O HOLY ONE ABOVE-
I AM TRULY GRATEFUL FOR YOUR BLOOD OF LIFE AND LOVE.
FOR HOLY AND TRUE-
IS MY SINCERE LOVE FOR YOU.
FOR I NO LONGER WORRY, YOU SEE-
FOR I TRULY LOVE AND TRUST HOLY THEE.
FOR GRACIOUS, KIND AND TRUE-
ARE THE HOLY GIFTS THAT COME WITH BLESSED LIFE SAVING YOU.
I DO NOT WORRY-
FOR THE LOVE OF MY LIFE (CHRIST JESUS) DESCENDED TO ME FROM HEAVEN'S REALM OF UNENDING GLORY.

HOLY AND TRUE-
ARE THE OPEN ARMS OF LOVE THAT COME FROM **LIFE GIVING AND REWARDING YOU.**
HOLY, HOLY, HOLY-
IS THE BLOOD THAT COMFORTS AND SURROUNDS **BLESSED AND TRUSTING ME.**
HOLY AND TRUE-
IS THE PRECIOUS BLOOD THAT **DESCENDED WITH ETERNAL YOU.**
I DO NOT WORRY,
FOR I AM IN THE HOLY PRESENCE AND CARE OF *CHRIST JESUS,* **THE EVERLASTING KING OF GLORY.**
OH DIVINE **BLOOD OF LOVE-**
I PRAISE YOU FOR DESCENDED WITHIN THE PHYSICAL BODY OF *CHRIST JESUS,* **FROM SWEET HEAVEN ABOVE.**
HOLY, HOLY, HOLY ARE YOU,
O PRECIOUS BLOOD THAT IS **LIFE SAVING AND TRUE.**
MARCH 23, 2019

THE SACRIFICIAL LAMB'S *BLOOD AND ME*

BARBARA SPEAKING

HOLY IS THE **BLOOD AND ME-**
HOLY IS THE PRECIOUS **BLOOD OF CHRIST, THE ALMIGHTY.**
FOR **CHOSEN, YOU SEE-**
IS THE BRIDE (BARBARA) OF THE **SACRIFICIAL LAMB OF GOD ALMIGHTY.**
FOR THE **SACRED BLOOD OF LOVE-**
DESCENDED TO ME FROM **SWEET HEAVEN ABOVE.**
HOLY, YOU SEE-
ARE *CHRIST JESUS'* **PRECIOUS BLOOD AND BLESSED ME.**
FOR **GOD'S BLOOD OF LIFE-**
DWELLS WITHIN ME, **HIS CHOSEN AND SENT MESSENGER AND WIFE.**
HOLY AND TRUE-
IS THE PRECIOUS LIFE SAVING BLOOD THAT **I DELIVER TO YOU.**
FOR **GRACE AND MERCY-**
SHINE FROM THE SACRED BLOOD THAT WAS SHED ON SWEET CALVARY, BY **CHRIST ALMIGHTY.**

BARBARA ANN MARY MACK

HOLY, YOU SEE-
ARE THE BLOOD OF *CHRIST JESUS AND BLESSED PURIFIED ME.*
MARCH 24, 2019

YES, I WILL FOLLOW THE PRECIOUS BLOOD OF CHRIST JESUS, AS HE LEAVES THE BATTLEFIELD OF VICTORY AND EVER-LASTING FAME

BARBARA SPEAKING

YES! YES! YES!
I WILL FOLLOW THE *TRIUMPHANT BLOOD OF CHRIST JESUS!*
FOR *HOLY, YOU SEE-*
IS THE *BLOOD OF VICTORY!*
HOLY AND TRUE-
IS THE BATTLE ON SWEET CALVARY THAT WAS *WON BY THE TRIUMPHANT SACRIFICIAL ACT OF LOVING YOU.*
THE SACRED BATTLE ON *SWEET CALVARY-*
WAS WON BY THE TRIUMPHANT SACRIFICIAL ACT OF *CHRIST ALMIGHTY.*
YES, I WILL FOLLOW THE *LIFE SAVING BLOOD-*
THAT GRACED US WITH THE PRESENCE OF *JESUS' SACRIFICIAL ACT OF DIVINE UNENDING LOVE.*
FOR *HOLY AND REAL-*
IS THE LOVE THAT WE CAN *TRULY SEE AND FEEL!*
HOLY AND TRUE-
IS THE PRECIOUS BLOOD THAT *SAVES ME AND YOU.*
YES, I WILL FOLLOW, *YOU SEE-*
THE HOLY BLOOD OF *SWEET VICTORY!*
FOR *HOLY, YOU SEE-*
IS THE BLOOD THAT PIERCED THE SOULS AT *SWEET CALVARY.*
MARCH 24, 2019

IT IS TRUE

BARBARA SPEAKING

IT IS TRUE-
CHRIST JESUS, THE SACRIFICED ONE, DID SHED HIS LIFE SAVING BLOOD FOR ME AND YOU.
HOLY, YOU SEE-
IS THE GOD WHO DIED ON THE CROSS OF LOVE FOR YOU AND ME.
CAN YOU NOT SEE-
THAT THE LAMB OF GOD, TRULY LOVES BLESSED THEE?
FOR IT IS TRUE AND REAL-
YOUR SAVED SOULS, SATAN, THE DEVIL, CAN NO LONGER STEAL!
FOR HOLY AND TRUE, YOU SEE-
IS THE SACRIFICIAL BLOOD THAT SAVED AND REMOVED YOU FROM THE WORLD OF SIN THAT CAPTURED THEE.
FOR HOLY IS THE BLOOD-
THAT REMOVED YOUR SINS BY THE POWER OF DIVINELY SENT LOVE.
IT IS TRUE-
THAT HE, CHRIST JESUS, DIED ON THE HOLY CROSS OF LOVE FOR SINFUL ME AND YOU.
IT IS TRUE, YOU SEE-
THAT HE SUFFERED TREMENDOUSLY FOR YOU AND ME.
FOR SALVATION-
IS FOR EVERY REPENTANT NATION.
SALVATION THROUGH CHRIST JESUS-
IS A DIVINE HEAVENLY GIFT THAT IS OFFERED TO BLESSED US.
FOR HOLY, YOU SEE-
IS THE BLOOD THAT SAVES REPENTANT YOU AND ME.
HOLY AND REAL-
IS THE BLOOD THAT SATAN CANNOT ENTER NOR STEAL.
HOLY AND REAL-
IS THE HEAVENLY LOVE THAT I CAN TRULY SEE AND FEEL.
RIGHTEOUS, RIGHTEOUS, RIGHTEOUS-

BARBARA ANN MARY MACK

IS THE LIFE SAVING BLOOD THAT WAS SHED ON SWEET CALVARY, BY **OUR LORD AND SAVIOR, CHRIST** JESUS.

MARCH 24, 2019

MARY, THE BLESSED MOTHER OF CHRIST JESUS, THE SACRIFICIAL LAMB OF GOD ALMIGHTY

YOUR (CHRIST JESUS) PAIN: MY PAIN: MY LOVE, SAYS BLESSED MARY AND BARBARA ANN MARY MACK, THE SACRIFICIAL LAMB OF GOD'S EVERLASTING BRIDE

BLESSED MARY AND BARBARA SPEAKING TO THE SCOURGED AND CRUCIFIED LORD JESUS

YOUR PAIN, **LORD JESUS**-
IS THE PAIN THAT TORMENTS **BLESSED US** (MARY, THE MOTHER OF CHRIST JESUS AND BARBARA).
YOUR SUFFERING AND AGONY-
HAVE CAUSED OUR (BLESSED MARY AND BARBARA) SOULS AND SPIRITS TO WEEP IN THE HOLY PRESENCE OF **GOD, OUR HEAVENLY FATHER; THE ALMIGHTY**.
YOUR MANY TEARS, **LORD JESUS**-
HAVE **CARRIED US** (BLESSED MARY AND BARBARA).
FOR **HOLY IS HE** (CHRIST JESUS)-
WHO SUFFERED IN THE HOLY PRESENCE OF **GOD, THE FATHER, BARBARA AND BLESSED ME** (MARY, THE MOTHER OF CHRIST JESUS).

BARBARA SPEAKING TO JESUS, THE CRUCIFIED AND VICTORIOUS SACRIFICIAL LAMB OF GOD

MY HOLY **SPOUSE AND GOD**-
I BLESS YOU FOR **YOUR SACRIFICE AND LOVE**.
FOR HOLY AND **FAITHFUL ARE YOU**-
TO YOUR CHOSEN BRIDE (BARBARA), WHO IS **FAITHFUL AND TRUE**.
FOR, I BOW **MY ANOINTED HEAD**-
IN THE HOLY PRESENCE OF HE (CHRIST JESUS) HAS BEEN **RAISED FROM THE DEAD**.
HOLY IS HE (CHRIST JESUS)-
WHO SUFFERED TREMENDOUSLY FOR THE **WORTHY AND THE FREE**.
BLESSED AND **HOLY IS HE** (CHRIST JESUS)-

who endured much pain for *GOD, THE FATHER, YOUR BLESSED CHOSEN MOTHER AND ME.*
HOLY IS HE (CHRIST JESUS)-
whose precious and priceless blood pierced the wood and ground as *he hung on sweet Calvary.*
March 5, 2019

I HAVE WITNESSED THE BRUTAL BEATINGS AND HORRORS OF MY SON'S SACRIFICIAL ACT OF LOVE, *SAYS MARY, JESUS' EARTHLY MOTHER.*

THE BLESSED MARY SPEAKING

MAKE IT STOP! MAKE IT STOP!
Make the brutal beatings cease before *MY BELOVED SON'S HEAD AND SPIRIT DROP!*
For I have witnessed, *YOU SEE-*
The evil abusers *BRUTALITY.*
I AM AN EYE WITNESS-
To the brutal beating and crucifixion of *MY BELOVED SON, CHRIST JESUS.*
My heart and soul felt *EVERY BEATING-*
That tortured the holy body of my son, *THE ROYAL AND HOLY EVERLASTING KING.*
MAKE HIS AGONY STOP-
Before my blessed *SPIRIT AND BODY DROP.*
March 5, 2019

BEHOLD MY PRESENT TESTAMENT

STOP HURTING MY SON, SAYS MARY, THE MOTHER OF CHRIST JESUS

MARY, THE MOTHER OF CHRIST JESUS, SPEAKING

STOP HURTING THE HOLY ONE WHOM I LOVE-
FOR HE, THE LORD JESUS, DESCENDED TO ME FROM HEAVEN ABOVE.
HE WAS SENT WITH THE GIFT OF LIFE,
SO THAT WE MAY BE REMOVED FROM WORLDLY STRIFE.
STOP HURTING MY SON, CHRIST ALMIGHTY,
FOR HE IS THE GIFT OF LOVE THAT WAS GIVEN TO BLESSED ME.
LET ME ENDURE THE PAIN AND SUFFERING-
INSTEAD OF MY SON, CHRIST, THE ETERNAL KING.
FOR HOLY IS MY SON (CHRIST JESUS)-
WHO BECAME A SACRIFICE FOR EVERYONE.
HOLY AND ETERNAL IS HE (CHRIST JESUS)-
WHO WAS PLACED IN MY EARTHLY CARE BY GOD, THE FATHER; THE ALMIGHTY.
MARCH 5, 2019

IT IS FINISHED, MY SON, SAYS MARY, JESUS' EARTHLY MOTHER OF DIVINE LOVE

MARY, JESUS' EARTHLY MOTHER OF DIVINE LOVE, SPEAKING

IT IS FINISHED, MY SON,
FOR YOUR DIVINE WORK ON EARTH IS FINALLY DONE.
YOU HAVE FINISHED ON EARTH-
THE DIVINE ASSIGNMENT THAT ACCOMPANIED YOUR HOLY PHYSICAL BIRTH.
YOU MAY NOW REST IN SWEET HEAVEN ABOVE,
AS YOU SHARE WITH YOUR HEAVENLY FATHER, HIS REALM OF UNENDING LOVE.
FOR HOLY IS HE (GOD, THE FATHER)-
WHO HAS SENT HE (CHRIST JESUS) WHO IS PURE AND WORTHY.
IT IS FINISHED, MY LOVE (CHRIST JESUS)-
AND NOW, YOU RESIDE IN YOUR GLORY, IN SWEET HEAVEN ABOVE.
IT IS FINISHED, MY SON (CHRIST JESUS);
AND NOW, YOU RESIDE IN SWEET PARADISE WITH ALMIGHTY GOD, THE ETERNAL HOLY ONE.
IT IS FINISHED! IT IS FINISHED!

AND NOW, YOU CAN REJOICE WITH THE REALM (ALMIGHTY GOD, THE FATHER) THAT SENT YOU TO THE NEEDY AND SINFUL **REALM OF THE WOUNDED.**

MARCH 5, 2019

WEEP WITH ME, DEAR MOTHER, *SAYS THE SCOURGED AND CRUCIFIED LORD JESUS*

<u>THE SCOURGED AND CRUCIFIED LORD *JESUS* SPEAKING TO MARY, HIS MOTHER</u>

WEEP WITH ME, **O BLESSED MOTHER-**
WEEP IN THE PRESENCE OF **MY EARTHLY SISTER AND BROTHER.**
WEEP WITH ME,
SO THAT THE **WORLD MAY SEE.**
THEY WILL WITNESS THE **PAIN AND GLORY-**
THAT COME WITH THE SACRIFICIAL ACT OF **CHRIST ALMIGHTY.**
THEY WILL SEE-
THE BLESSED MOTHER WHO **NURTURED HOLY ME.**
WEEP, DEAR MOTHER-
AS YOU REVEAL MY DIVINE PURPOSE **TO THE OTHER.**
FOR IT IS TIME, **DEAR MOTHER-**
TO REVEAL THE TRUTH THAT DESCENDED WITH ME FROM **GOD, OUR HEAVENLY FATHER.**

MARCH 5, 2019

AND I COULD NOT DO NOR SAY ANYTHING, *SAYS MARY, THE MOTHER OF THE CRUCIFIED CHRIST JESUS*

<u>MARY, THE MOTHER OF THE CRUCIFIED CHRIST *JESUS,* SPEAKING</u>

I STOOD SILENT, AND IN **GREAT AGONY,**
FOR I KNEW THAT *CHRIST,* MY SON, CAME TO **SAVE AND SANCTIFY THE SINFUL WORLD AND ME.**
I COULD NOT **RELEASE A SOUND;**
FOR I KNEW THAT **GOD, OUR FATHER, WAS AROUND.**
FOR HE GAVE ME THE STRENGTH, **YOU SEE-**

TO WITNESS AND ENDURE THE ABUSE THAT WAS PLACED ON **MY SON, CHRIST ALMIGHTY**.
I COULD NOT SPEAK OR **SAY A WORD**,
BUT I KNEW THAT MY PAIN AND **AGONY WERE HEARD**.
FOR GOD, OUR **HEAVENLY FATHER ABOVE**,
SACRIFICED FOR US, **HIS GREATEST LOVE** (CHRIST JESUS).
MARCH 5, 2019

MY BODY, SPIRIT AND SOUL TREMBLED WITH PAIN AT THE SIGHT OF MY BELOVED SON'S EXECUTION AND DEATH ON THE CROSS, SAYS MARY, CHRIST JESUS' CHOSEN MOTHER

MARY, CHRIST JESUS' CHOSEN MOTHER, SPEAKING

MY ENTIRE BODY-
TREMBLED AT THE EXECUTION OF **MY SON AND HOLY GOD, CHRIST ALMIGHTY**.
FOR, I DID SEE-
THE CRUCIFIED KING OF KINGS WHO **DIED ON HOLY CALVARY**.
I DID WITNESS-
MY SON'S **HOLY POSITION AND GOODNESS**.
MY SPIRIT TREMBLED WITH **GRIEF AND AGONY**-
AT THE EXECUTION OF MY **BELOVED SON, CHRIST ALMIGHTY**.
FOR HOLY IS HE (CHRIST JESUS)-
WHO WAS EXECUTED ON **SWEET CALVARY**.
HOLY AND **EVERLASTING IS HE** (CHRIST JESUS)-
WHO WAS EXECUTED FOR **BLESSED YOU AND ME**.
MARCH 5, 2019

AND I REMAINED OPENLY SILENT, *SAYS MARY, THE BLESSED MOTHER OF CHRIST JESUS*

THE BLESSED MOTHER OF THE CRUCIFIED LORD JESUS, SPEAKING

My lips remain *sealed with pain and agony,*
As I witness the brutality and torture of *my holy son, Christ Jesus, the Almighty.*
For He kept my soul silent *during His beating,*
As I witnessed the suffering of *my holy Lord and King.*
My spirit *wept without ceasing,*
As my eyes beheld the pain that covered the precious face of *Christ, my son and holy King.*
For I could not speak or *cry out,*
As my wounded spirit *leapt and shout.*

March 5, 2019

MY HOLY SON'S, CHRIST JESUS, PAIN AND AGONY, ECHO THROUGH MY HEART AND MY TOTAL BEING, *SAYS MARY, JESUS' EARTHLY MOTHER*

MARY, JESUS' EARTHLY MOTHER SPEAKING TO THE SCOURGED AND CRUCIFIED LORD JESUS

I can feel it, my son.
I can feel the agony that has engulfed *the divine being of Christ, the Holy One.*
I can feel *the joyless body-*
Yes, the holy being of *Christ Almighty.*
For your *pain and agony-*
Have engulfed the spirit and soul of *chosen me.*
My son: your endless physical pain has *surrounded me.*
It has surrounded the blessed mother whom *our Heavenly Father has given to thee.*

March 5, 2019

BLESSED IS MARY, THE EARTHLY MOTHER OF CHRIST JESUS, THE SACRIFICIAL LAMB OF ALMIGHTY GOD, THE FATHER

BARBARA SPEAKING TO BLESSED MARY, THE EARTHLY MOTHER OF CHRIST JESUS, THE SACRIFICIAL LAMB OF ALMIGHTY GOD, THE FATHER

BLESSED! BLESSED! *BLESSED IS THEE*-
BLESSED IS *MARY*, THE MOTHER OF *CHRIST ALMIGHTY*.
FOR *HOLY AND TRUE*-
IS THE LIVING BLOOD THAT HAS SAVED *CHOSEN AND WORTHY YOU*.
HOLY AND *CHOSEN, YOU SEE*-
IS THE EARTHLY MOTHER OF *CHRIST, THE ALMIGHTY*.
HOLY IS THE *BLOOD OF CHRIST JESUS*-
HOLY AND CHOSEN IS THE BLESSED MOTHER WHO *LIVED AMONG US*.
FOR SHE WAS *CHOSEN, YOU SEE*-
BY *CHRIST JESUS, AND GOD, THE FATHER; YES, SWEET ETERNITY!*
BLESSED AND CHOSEN IS THE MOTHER OF *CHRIST JESUS, THE SACRIFICIAL LAMB OF GOD*.
FOREVER IS SHE WHO NOW LIVES WITH GOD, IN *SWEET PARADISE ABOVE*.
FOR *HOLY IS SHE*-
WHO DID BEAR, WITH DIVINE GIVEN FAITH, THE *EVER-LIVING CHRIST JESUS; THE ALMIGHTY*.
MARCH 24, 2019

PRAISE AND THE SACRIFICIAL BLOOD OF CHRIST JESUS, THE LAMB OF GOD

REJOICING IN THE MIDST OF CHRIST JESUS' LIFE SAVING BLOOD

BARBARA SPEAKING

REJOICE! REJOICE! REJOICE, O PRECIOUS **BLOOD OF CHRIST JESUS!**
REJOICE, O BLESSED BLOOD, AS MY SPIRIT DANCES IN THE HOLY PRESENCE OF THE SACRIFICIAL LAMB WHO **SAVES US!**
FOR WE, THE BELIEVING ONES, ARE TRULY GRATEFUL TO **CHRIST, OUR EVERLASTING KING.**
AND WE WILL REJOICE AS OUR BLESSED SPIRITS **DANCE AND SING!**
OUR **SONGS OF PRAISE-**
WILL GOVERN **OUR BLESSED DAYS!**
HALLELUJAH! HALLELUJAH-
TO **ALMIGHTY GOD JEHOVAH!!!**
MARCH 8, 2019

REJOICING WITHIN THE KINGDOM THAT IS *RULED BY THE PRECIOUS BLOOD OF CHRIST JESUS, THE SACRIFICIAL LAMB OF GOD*

BARBARA SPEAKING TO THE REJOICING ONES

REJOICE! REJOICE!
REJOICE, DEAR BROTHERS AND SISTERS, AS YOU LIFT YOUR **GRATEFUL UNIFIED VOICE!**
REJOICE IN THE MIDST OF THE HOLY BLOOD OF **THE SACRIFICED ONE (CHRIST JESUS)!**
REJOICE IN THE MIDST OF THE PRECIOUS BLOOD OF *CHRIST JESUS*, **GOD, THE FATHER'S, ONLY BEGOTTEN SON.**
EXHIBIT THE JOY-
THAT COMES FROM THE SPIRIT AND SOUL OF THE **SACRIFICIAL LAMB'S WORTHY GIRL AND BOY.**
REJOICE IN THE PRESENCE OF **ALMIGHTY GOD'S DIVINE LOVE,**
AS YOU BOW IN THE MIDST OF **HIS LIFE SAVING BLOOD.**
HOLY, HOLY, **HOLY IS HE** (CHRIST *JESUS*)-
WHO HAS SHED HIS PRECIOUS AND PRICELESS BLOOD FOR **YOU AND ME!**
MARCH 9, 2019

O HOLY BLOOD OF *CHRIST JESUS*, YOU ARE WORTHY TO BE PRAISED!

BARBARA SPEAKING TO THE HOLY BLOOD OF CHRIST *JESUS*

OH HOLY BLOOD OF **DIVINE MERCY AND LOVE-**
YOU ARE WORTHY TO BE PRAISED, FOR YOU FLOW FROM THE BODY OF *CHRIST JESUS*, THE HOLY ONE, WHO DESCENDED TO US FROM **SWEET HEAVEN ABOVE.**
HOLY AND TRUE-
ARE **EVER-FLOWING YOU.**
FOR YOU, **O SANCTIFYING BLOOD-**
REVEAL THE PRESENCE OF **SACRIFICIAL LOVE.**
HOLY AND TRUE-
ARE **EVER-FLOWING YOU.**
MY BODY AND SOUL **SING PRAISE-**
TO YOU, THROUGHOUT MY **BLESSED GOD SENT DAYS.**

For *holy and true*-
Are the blessings that come with knowing, loving, and *dancing with you*.
Holy and true-
Are the good things for us that *you, every day, do*.
Worthy, worthy, worthy-
Is the precious life saving blood of *Christ Almighty!!!*

March 16, 2019

The holy blood of *Christ Jesus*, the sacrificial lamb of God, has removed the tears from my weeping eyes and soul. And now, *my blessed spirit sings songs of praise to the blood of the lamb of God*. *Hallelujah!!!*

Barbara Speaking

The precious blood of *my living God*,
Has removed the many tears from *my weeping spirit and eyes*.
For holy is the blood that *belongs to He* (Christ *Jesus, the sacrificial lamb of God, the Father*)-
Who has comforted *weeping me*.
The precious holy *blood of Christ Jesus*-
Removes the hurt and pain that *follows believing and faithful us*.
The precious blood has *removed within*-
The filth and destruction of our *inner sin*.
For *holy is He* (Christ *Jesus*)-
Who removes the tears that have conquered wounded and *vulnerable you and me*.
Praise! Praise! Praise!
Fills my blessed *God ordered rejoicing days!*
For *holy is the blood*-
That showers my soul with *divine sent love*.
I will weep no more,
For the precious blood of the sacrificial lamb of God, has led me through *heaven's open door*.

March 17, 2019

LISTEN TO THE VOICES OF PRAISE AS GOD'S HOLY ANGELS *BOW IN THE HOLY PRESENCE OF THE BLOOD OF THE LAMB OF GOD*

GOD'S HOLY ANGELS SPEAKING

LISTEN TO *OUR VOICES OF PRAISE,*
AS WE BOW IN THE PRESENCE OF THE LAMB'S BLOOD THROUGHOUT *OUR ENDLESS DAYS.*
PRAISE! PRAISE! PRAISE-
IN THE MIDST OF OUR *WORSHIPPING DAYS!*
FOR THE BLOOD OF *THE LAMB OF GOD-*
EXHIBITS TO US, THE PRESENCE OF *DIVINE LIGHT AND LOVE.*
FOR *HOLY IS THE BLOOD-*
THAT RELEASES GOD'S SACRIFICIAL ACT OF *UNENDING AND UNSELFISH MERCY AND LOVE.*
SING! SING! SING!
LET OUR REJOICING SONGS UNITE WITH THE HEAVENLY BELLS AS *THEY RING!*
MARCH 17, 2019

REJOICING WITH *THE SACRED BLOOD OF THE LAMB OF ALMIGHTY GOD, EVERY DAY!*

BARBARA SPEAKING

REJOICE! REJOICE!
LIFT YOUR *PRAISING UNIFIED VOICE!*
REJOICE WITH THE SACRIFICIAL *BLOOD OF CHRIST JESUS!*
REJOICE IN THE HOLY PRESENCE OF HE WHO SACRIFICED HIS PRECIOUS LIFE FOR *ALL OF US!*
FOR *HOLY AND TRUE-*
IS THE PRICELESS BLOOD THAT SEES *THE BELIEVING ONES THROUGH!*
REJOICE IN THE MIDST OF *THE BELIEVING ONES!*
REJOICE WITH THE PRECIOUS BLOOD OF THE SLAUGHTERED LAMB OF GOD, O *PRAISING DAUGHTERS AND SONS!*
FOR IT IS TRUE-

THAT *CHRIST,* THE LAMB OF ALMIGHTY GOD, SACRIFICED HIS PRECIOUS BLOOD AND LIFE FOR *ME AND YOU.*
REJOICE, O *BLESSED BROTHERS!*
SING SONGS OF PRAISE, O *WORTHY SISTERS!*
FOR THE BLOOD OF *WORTHY CHRIST JESUS-*
SINGS IN THE MIDST OF *BLESSED AND WORTHY US!*
HALLELUJAH!!! HALLELUJAH!!!
SING SONGS OF PRAISE TO THE SACRIFICIAL LAMB OF *ALMIGHTY GOD, THE FATHER, JEHOVAH!!!*
MARCH 17, 2019

LET ALL OF THE BELIEVING SOULS REJOICE EVERY DAY, IN THE HOLY PRESENCE OF THE SACRIFICIAL LAMB OF GOD'S LIFE SAVING BLOOD

BARBARA SPEAKING

O BELIEVING ONES-
O BLESSED *DAUGHTERS AND SONS!*
LET US *REJOICE TODAY-*
AS WE FOLLOW THE SACRIFICIAL *LAMB'S HOLY WAY!*
LET US REJOICE IN THE *MIDST OF THE BLOOD-*
THAT EXPRESSES FOR US, *TRUE AND UNCONDITIONAL LOVE.*
FOR, *HOLY, HOLY, HOLY-*
IS THE BLOOD OF THE SACRIFICIAL LAMB, *CHRIST ALMIGHTY.*
LET OUR *BLESSED SOULS REJOICE!*
LET US LIFT OUR *PRAISING UNITED VOICE!*
FOR *TOGETHER WE STAND-*
IN THE MIDST OF *GOD'S HOLY LAND.*
REJOICE, *O BLESSED SPIRIT!*
REJOICE, SO THAT *ALL MAY HEAR IT!*
WE ARE *TRULY GLAD-*
FOR WE ARE REMOVED FROM THE *SIN THAT WE ONCE HAD.*
REJOICE! REJOICE! REJOICE!
LET THE BELIEVING ONES *UNITE IN ONE HOLY VOICE.*
FOR, *HOLY AND TRUE-*
IS THE LAMB'S BLOOD THAT WAS SHED FOR ME AND *BLESSED REDEEMED YOU.*

HALLELUJAH!!!
MARCH 17, 2019

HOLY IS THE SOUND OF ENDLESS PRAISE UNTO THE PRECIOUS BLOOD OF CHRIST JESUS, THE SACRIFICIAL SLAUGHTERED LAMB OF GOD

BARBARA SPEAKING

HOLY IS *THE ENDLESS SOUND*-
THAT REJOICES IN THE MIDST OF THE LIFE SAVING HOLY BLOOD THAT IS *ALWAYS AROUND.*
REJOICE, O HOLY SOUNDS OF PRAISE! REJOICE IN THE HOLY PRESENCE OF *ALMIGHTY GOD JEHOVAH!*
RELEASE, EVERYONE, THE *MAGNIFICENT SOUND OF HALLELUJAH!*
FOR HOLY IS *THE FATHER AND GOD*-
OF CHRIST JESUS, THE *SACRIFICIAL SON OF LOVE.*
HOLY IS THE *BLOOD OF HE (CHRIST JESUS)*-
WHO SACRIFICED HIS PRECIOUS LIFE FOR *YOU AND ME.*
MARCH 17, 2019

THROUGH THE WINDOW OF DIVINE LOVE

BARBARA SPEAKING

LOOK THROUGH THE *WINDOW OF LOVE*-
THERE, YOU WILL SEE THE DWELLING PLACE CALLED *SWEET HEAVEN ABOVE.*
FOR *HOLY, YOU SEE*-
IS THE DIVINE WINDOW OF SWEET HEAVEN, AS ALMIGHTY GOD AND HEAVEN'S BLESSED RESIDENTS, *WELCOME BLESSED ME.*
THROUGH THE DIVINE WINDOW, I CAN SEE *GOD'S HEAVENLY ANGELS ON HIGH*-
AS THEY SING SONGS OF PRAISE TO THE HOLY ONE, WHO SITS ON *HIS MIGHTY THRONE ABOVE THE BLUE SKY.*
FOR *HOLY, YOU SEE*-
IS THE DIVINE PLACE *(HEAVEN)* THAT *WELCOMES ME.*
HOLY, YOU SEE-
IS THE DIVINE WINDOW OF LOVE THAT *LEADS TO GOD ALMIGHTY.*

FOR THROUGH *THE WINDOW OF LOVE*-
I CAN SEE THE SACRIFICIAL *LAMB'S LIFE SAVING BLOOD.*
FOR *HOLY IS HE* (CHRIST *JESUS*)-
WHO SITS ON HIS MIGHTY THRONE IN THE PRESENCE OF *INVITED AND BLESSED ME.*
MARCH 22, 2019

REJOICING WITH *THE HOLY BLOOD THAT SAVES US*

BARBARA SPEAKING

REJOICING WITH THE PRECIOUS BLOOD OF *THE LAMB THAT SAVES US.*

YES, I AM REJOICING WITH THE PRICELESS LIVING BLOOD OF *VICTORIOUS CHRIST JESUS*!
FOR *HOLY IS HE* (CHRIST *JESUS*)-
WHOSE BLOOD HAS *CLEANSED AND SAVED BLESSED YOU AND ME.*
HOLY AND TRUE-
IS THE LIFE SAVING BLOOD THAT HAS *CAPTURED ME AND YOU.*
REJOICE! REJOICE! REJOICE!
LET *CHRIST*, OUR SACRIFICIAL GOD, *HEAR OUR UNITED VOICE!*
FOR *HOLY AND TRUE*-
IS THE GOD WHO HAS *BLESSED ME AND PRAISING YOU!*
MARCH 24, 2019

BEHOLD MY PRESENT TESTAMENT

"Volume Thirty-Four"

"My Glory"

BY:

BARBARA ANN MARY MACK

BEGAN: MARCH 29, 2019

COMPLETED: MARCH 29, 2019

CONTENTS

Dedication 158
Acknowledgment 159
Introduction 160
Behold *My Glory* 163

DEDICATION

TO: *CHRIST JESUS,* THE GLORIOUS AND ONLY BEGOTTEN SON OF GOD, THE FATHER

ACKNOWLEDGMENT

HE, *CHRIST JESUS*, IS GOD, THE FATHER'S, REALM OF GLORY, WHO DESCENDS TO US EVERY DAY.

INTRODUCTION

HOLY, HOLY, **HOLY IS HE** (CHRIST JESUS)—
WHO DESCENDS TO **THOSE WHO ARE WORTHY.**
MARCH 29, 2019

DIVINE GLORY: CHRIST JESUS

ALMIGHTY GOD, THE FATHER, JEHOVAH, SPEAKING OF CHRIST JESUS, HIS ONLY BEGOTTEN SON

HIS RADIANCE AND GLORY SHINE,
BECAUSE **HE IS ALL MINE!**
DIVINE GLORY IS HE (CHRIST JESUS)—
FOR HIS HOLY ESSENCE AND PRESENCE CAME FROM **ETERNAL ME** (JEHOVAH GOD, THE FATHER).
HOLY, YOU SEE—
IS THE ONE (CHRIST JESUS) WHO IS **FUSED WITH ETERNAL HOLY ME.**
FOR **CHRIST JESUS, MY BELOVED SON**—
ENTERED EXISTENCE BEFORE **THE HUMAN ONE.**
HOLY AND TRUE—
IS THE GLORIOUS ONE (CHRIST JESUS) WHO CAME **BEFORE HE AND I CREATED YOU.**
ETERNAL AND EVERLASTING—
IS THE GLORIOUS **CHRIST, THE LIVING SON AND KING.**
MARCH 29, 2019

THE GLORY OF CHRIST JESUS, GOD, THE FATHER'S, ONLY BEGOTTEN SON

ALMIGHTY GOD, THE FATHER, JEHOVAH, SPEAKING OF CHRIST JESUS, HIS ONLY BEGOTTEN SON

GLORY, GLORY, GLORY-
SURROUNDS MY BELOVED CHRIST ALMIGHTY!
FOR HE (CHRIST JESUS)-
REIGNS WITH ETERNAL ME.
MY ONLY BEGOTTEN SON (CHRIST JESUS)-
IS THE ETERNAL BELOVED ONE.
FOR HOLY, YOU SEE-
IS THE ONLY SON WHO CAME FROM BLESSED ME.
RECEIVE MY GLORY (CHRIST JESUS)-
RECEIVE CHRIST JESUS, MY ONLY BEGOTTEN UNENDING LOVE STORY.
FOR HOLY AND TRUE-
IS THE GLORIOUS ONE (CHRIST JESUS) WHO CALLS BLESSED YOU.
SEEK, DEAR ONES-
SEEK CHRIST JESUS, THE GLORIOUS ONE, O BLESSED DAUGHTERS AND SONS.
FOR HE (CHRIST JESUS)-
TRULY SEEKS BLESSED THEE.
MARCH 29, 2019

MY GLORIOUS KINGDOM (CHRIST JESUS), SAYS JEHOVAH GOD, THE FATHER

JEHOVAH GOD, THE FATHER, SPEAKING

MY ONLY BEGOTTEN SON-
YES, CHRIST JESUS, THE RULER, AND MY GLORIOUS HEAVENLY AND EARTHLY KINGDOM.
HOLY IS HE (CHRIST JESUS)-
WHO BRINGS GLORY TO YOU AND ME.
HOLY IS THE ONE (CHRIST JESUS)-
YES, CHRIST JESUS, MY ONLY BEGOTTEN SON.
HOLY AND TRUE-
IS THE LOVE OF THE KINGDOM (CHRIST JESUS) THAT I HAVE SENT TO YOU.

FOR *HOLY AND TRUE*-
IS *CHRIST JESUS,* THE BLESSED KINGDOM THAT *I HAVE GIVEN TO YOU.*
MY SON (*CHRIST JESUS*)-
MY KINGDOM OF LOVE WHO DESCENDS EVERY DAY TO *THE BELIEVING ONE.*
FOR *HOLY AND REAL*-
IS THE KINGDOM'S (*CHRIST JESUS*) PRESENCE THAT THE BELIEVING ONES *CAN FEEL.*
HOLY AND TRUE-
IS THE MIGHTY KINGDOM (*CHRIST JESUS*) WHO DESCENDS FROM *MY ARMS OF LOVE TO BLESSED YOU.*
REACH FOR HIM TODAY-
REACH FOR MY HOLY KINGDOM (*CHRIST JESUS*) DEAR CHILDREN, AS YOU *SEEK AND FIND HIS LIFE SAVING WAY.*
FOR *HOLY AND REAL*-
IS THE KINGDOM (*CHRIST JESUS*) THAT THE EVIL ONES *CANNOT ENTER NOR STEAL.*
MARCH 29, 2019

BEHOLD *MY GLORY*

BEHOLD MY GLORY, SAYS CHRIST JESUS, THE LIVING REALM OF DIVINE LOVE

CHRIST JESUS, THE LIVING GLORY, SPEAKING

BEHOLD MY GLORY:
BEHOLD AND WITNESS *MY HEAVENLY STORY.*
FOR *I, YOUR LORD AND GOD-*
HAVE COME TO RELEASE UPON THE EARTH, *MY REALM OF HEAVENLY LOVE.*
I HAVE COME, *YOU SEE-*
TO REVEAL MY ULTIMATE EXPRESSION OF *LOVE AND DIVINE MERCY.*
I HAVE COME *BEFORE YOU-*
SO THAT YOU MAY WITNESS AND FEEL THE GLORIOUS ONE, WHO IS *HOLY, ETERNAL AND TRUE.*
I HAVE COME IN YOUR BLESSED MIDST, *YOU SEE-*
TO REVEAL THE DEPTH AND BRILLIANCE OF ME, WHO IS *DIVINE SENT HEAVENLY MERCY AND GLORY.*
I HAVE COME IN YOUR *BLESSED MIDST TODAY-*
TO SHOW YOU THE PATH, TO THE REALITY OF *MY HOLY UNCHANGING LIFE SAVING WAY.*
I HAVE COME, *YOU SEE-*
TO SHOW YOU *MY FORM AND DIVINE BEAUTY.*
I HAVE COME, *YOU SEE-*
TO REVEAL TO MY LOVED ONES ON EARTH TODAY, THE GLORY THAT COMES FROM THE ESSENCE OF *CHRIST JESUS, WHO IS GOD ALMIGHTY.*
FOR, *HOLY, HOLY, HOLY-*
AM I, WHO IS *CHRIST JESUS,* YOUR *HEAVENLY KING OF EVERLASTING GLORY!*
COME, AND *ENTER ME-*
ENTER MY REALM OF *HEAVEN SENT GLORY!*
FOR IN THE MIDST OF *THIS WORLD OF GLOOM-*
I WILL LEAD THE BLESSED ONES TO *MY GLORIOUS UPPER ROOM.*
FOR, *HOLY, HOLY, HOLY-*
IS THE HEAVENLY HOME OF *CHRIST JESUS, THE ALMIGHTY!*
COME, *O BLESSED ONES!*
REJOICE IN THE MIDST OF MY GLORY, O *WORTHY DAUGHTERS AND SONS!*
FOR *HOLY AND TRUE-*

IS THE ESSENCE OF DIVINE LOVE *(CHRIST JESUS)* THAT **DESCENDED TO YOU!**
HOLY, ETERNAL AND RIGHTEOUS-
IS YOUR **LORD AND GOD, CHRIST JESUS!**
FOR **HOLY AND TRUE-**
IS THE GLORIOUS GOD WHO DESCENDED TO **BLESSED AND BELOVED YOU!**
HOLY, YOU SEE-
ARE THE LOVE AND **EXISTENCE OF GOD ALMIGHTY.**
LOOK UP TO ME-
FOR, I AM THE HOLY ONE WHO FORMED FROM THE DUST OF THE GROUND, **BLESSED AND WELL-LOVED THEE.**
HOLY AND REAL-
IS THE GLORIOUS GOD WHOM THE BELIEVING ONES SPIRITS **CAN SEE AND FEEL.**
HOLY AND **FOREVER LASTING-**
IS YOUR GLORIOUS **CHRIST, THE LIVING REIGNING KING.**
FOR IN YOUR **BLESSED MIDST-**
I DESCEND TO YOU WITH MY DIVINE POWER AND **GLORIOUS KISS.**
FOR HOLY AND ETERNAL, **YOU SEE-**
IS THE GLORIOUS ONE *(CHRIST JESUS)* WHO **CARES VERY MUCH FOR THEE.**
WITNESS! WITNESS! WITNESS!
WITNESS THE MERCY AND **GLORY OF CHRIST JESUS!**
FOR **HOLY IS HE** *(CHRIST JESUS)-*
YES, THE ONE WHO **SAVES BELIEVING THEE!**
WALK WITH ME-
WALK IN THE MIDST OF **MY DESCENDED GLORY.**
FOR **HOLY, ETERNAL AND TRUE-**
IS THE GLORIOUS ONE *(CHRIST JESUS)* WHO **REIGNS OVER YOU.**
MY CHILDREN-
YES, THOSE OF YOU FROM **EVERY NATION-**
ENTER **MY GLORY TODAY.**
ENTER, DEAR ONES, **MY LIFE SAVING HOLY WAY.**
FOR **HOLY, YOU SEE-**
IS THE WAY THAT LEADS TO **BLESSED LIFE SAVING ME.**
FOR **HOLY AND TRUE-**
IS THE GLORIOUS REALM *(CHRIST JESUS)* THAT CALLS AND **BECKONS ALL OF YOU.**

DEAR CHILDREN: VISIT WITH *MY GLORY AND SPIRIT.*
SING SONGS OF PRAISE, SO THAT *OUR HEAVENLY FATHER AND I CAN HEAR IT!*
FOR *HOLY AND TRUE-*
ARE THE PRAISING SONGS THAT COME FROM *FAITHFUL AND OBEDIENT YOU.*
HOLY AND REAL-
IS THE LOVE THAT *THE FATHER AND I FEEL.*
FOR *TRULY, TRULY, TRULY-*
YOUR SONGS OF PRAISE ARE *WELCOMED BY THE FATHER AND ME.*
COME, *O BLESSED ONES!*
REJOICE, *MY PRAISING DAUGHTERS AND SONS!*
FOR *HOLY, HOLY, HOLY-*
IS THE PRAISE WORTHY *CHRIST ALMIGHTY!*
GLORY AND SPIRITUAL FAME-
SURROUND *MY PRAISE WORTHY NAME.*
HOLY AND TRUE-
ARE PRAISING AND *FAITHFUL YOU.*
REJOICE! REJOICE! REJOICE!
LIFT UP YOUR *PRAISING UNIFIED VOICE.*
FOR, *HOLY, YOU SEE-*
IS THE GOD WHO *LISTENS TO PRAISING THEE.*
REJOICE, DEAR CHILDREN, IN *YOUR PROMISE LANDS!*
REJOICE, DEAR ONES, AS YOU LIFT UP YOUR *PRAISING HEARTS AND HANDS!*
FOR *HOLY, HOLY, HOLY-*
IS *CHRIST JESUS*, THE KING OF *HEAVENLY AND EARTHLY GLORY.*
GLORY, GLORY, GLORY HALLELUJAH!
ALL PRAISES GO UP TO *OUR HEAVENLY FATHER AND GOD JEHOVAH!!!*
FOR HOLY AND *ETERNAL, YOU SEE-*
IS THE FATHER AND GOD OF *BELOVED CHRIST ALMIGHTY.*
LOOK UP TO THE FATHER, FOR HE IS THE *GREAT AND HOLY ONE.*
LOOK UP TO HE, WHO CREATED *HIS PRAISING DAUGHTER AND SON.*
FOR *HOLY AND TRUE-*
IS THE FATHER AND GOD OF ME *(CHRIST JESUS)* AND *BLESSED YOU.*
PRAISE OUR HEAVENLY *GOD AND FATHER-*
AS YOUR REJOICING SPIRITS *SING AND GATHER!*
FOR *HOLY AND REAL-*

IS THE FATHER AND GOD WHO YOU, THE BELIEVING ONES, CAN **SEE AND FEEL!**
HOLY AND TRUE-
IS THE GLORY OF HE WHO **CREATED BLESSED YOU.**
HOLY, HOLY, HOLY-
IS MY REALM OF **CONTINUOUS GLORY!**
HOLY AND TRUE-
IS THE GLORIOUS FACE (CHRIST JESUS) THAT SHINES OVER **BELOVED AND OBEDIENT YOU.**
GLORY, GLORY, GLORY-
IS THE REALM THAT RELEASES THE MANY GIFTS OF **CHRIST ALMIGHTY.**
HOLY AND REAL-
IS THE GLORY THAT THE GATES OF DESTRUCTION AND DOOM CAN **NEVER STIFLE OR STEAL!**
MARCH 29, 2019

CHRIST JESUS: THE GLORY AND TRUTH THAT SHINES

BARBARA SPEAKING

THE GLORY OF CHRIST JESUS-
SHINES IN THE MIDST AND PRESENCE OF **BELIEVING US.**
FOR HOLY AND TRUE-
IS THE GLORIOUS GOD WHO **APPEARS TO BELIEVING ME AND YOU.**
HIS GLORY-
REVEALS TO US, THE UNENDING BEAUTY OF **HIS LIFE SAVING HOLY PRESENCE AND STORY.**
MARCH 29, 2019

SHINE! SHINE! *SHINE, IN THE MIDST OF THOSE WHO ARE THINE!*

BARBARA SPEAKING TO THE LORD JESUS
SHINE, *O GREAT AND HOLY ONE (CHRIST JESUS)*-
SHINE ON YOUR PRAISING *DAUGHTER AND SON!*
SHINE *YOUR HOLY GLORY*-
AS WE CLING TO THE GRACE THAT COMES FROM *YOUR HOLY PRESENCE AND STORY.*
FOR *HOLY AND TRUE*-
IS THE GRACE THAT *SHINES FROM GLORIOUS YOU.*
SHINE ON YOUR WORTHY *FLOCK OF LOVE TODAY,*
AS WE SEEK YOUR GLORY AND *LIFE SAVING HOLY WAY.*
FOR *ETERNAL AND TRUE*-
IS THE GRACE AND MERCY THAT *SEES US THROUGH.*
SHINE, SHINE, SHINE!
SHINE UPON *THOSE WHO ARE THINE!*
FOR *BLESSED ARE WE*-
WHO FOLLOWS THE HOLY VOICE AND TEACHINGS OF *CHRIST JESUS, THE ALMIGHTY.*
HOLY AND TRUE-
IS THE GLORIOUS KING WHO IS RULER OVER THOSE WHO BOW IN THE PRESENCE OF *FAITHFUL YOU.*
MARCH 29, 2019

IN THE MIDST OF YOUR GLORIOUS ESSENCE, *I WILL BOW, MY LORD GOD*

BARBARA SPEAKING TO THE LORD JESUS

IN THE MIDST OF *YOUR GLORIOUS ESSENCE,*
I WILL BOW IN *MY GOD HOLY PRESENCE.*
IN THE MIDST OF THIS *BLESSED PERIOD OF TIME*-
I WILL BOW IN THE MIDST OF *THE GLORY THAT IS THINE.*
FOR *HOLY AND TRUE*-
IS MY ALLEGIANCE TO *GLORIOUS LIFE SAVING YOU.*
I WILL BATHE IN THE MIDST OF *YOUR ESSENCE OF GLORY*-
AS I SHARE WITH MY LOVED ONES, THE GIFT OF *YOUR UNENDING LOVE STORY.*

FOR *HOLY AND TRUE*-
IS THE *GLORY THAT IS YOU.*
LET *YOUR HOLY BELLS RING*-
AS MY REJOICING *SPIRIT AND BODY SING!*
FOR *HOLY AND REAL*-
IS THE GREAT GLORY THAT *I CAN SEE AND FEEL!*
I CAN REALLY FEEL-
THE ONLY GOD WHO IS *HOLY, ETERNAL AND REAL!*
AND, *I CAN REALLY SEE*-
THE GLORY THAT *REVEALS BLESSED THEE.*
FOR *HOLY AND TRUE*-
IS THE FAITH AND LOVE THAT *I HAVE WITH BELOVED YOU.*
HOLY, HOLY, HOLY-
IS *CHRIST JESUS' WELL OF HEAVENLY GLORY.*
MARCH 29, 2019

DIVINE GLORY, CHRIST JESUS, WALKS IN OUR BLESSED MIDST TODAY

<u>BARBARA SPEAKING</u>
BEHOLD! BEHOLD! BEHOLD!
BEHOLD THE BEAUTY AND GLORY OF THE GOOD SHEPHERD AS HE LEADS *HIS VICTORIOUS FOLD!*
BEHOLD *HIS HOLY GLORY AND PRESENCE*-
FOR HIS ESSENCE OF DIVINE LOVE WALKS THROUGH MY OBEDIENT BODY, WHICH IS *HIS EARTHLY HOME AND RESIDENCE.*
FOR *HOLY AND TRUE*-
IS THE GLORY OF HE *(CHRIST JESUS)* WHO *SPEAKS TO ME AND YOU.*
GLORY, GLORY, GLORY HALLELUJAH!
ALL HONOR AND PRAISE GO TO *CHRIST JESUS,* THE OBEDIENT AND ONLY BEGOTTEN SON OF *ALMIGHTY GOD JEHOVAH!!!*
MARCH 29, 2019

DIVINE GLORY, CHRIST JESUS, HAS DESCENDED TO US AGAIN

BARBARA SPEAKING TO THE LORD JESUS

YOU, O **BLESSED AND HOLY ONE,**
HAVE DESCENDED AGAIN, TO YOUR WORTHY AND BELOVED **DAUGHTER AND SON.**
AND WE ARE **TRULY GRATEFUL-**
TO BE GRACED BY THE HOLY PRESENCE OF A LOVE THAT IS **GREAT AND WONDERFUL.**
HOLY AND TRUE-
IS THE GRACE THAT COMES WITH **BELOVED YOU.**
AND WE, THE BELIEVING ONES, ARE **BLESSED TO SEE-**
THE GLORY OF **CHRIST, THE ETERNAL ALMIGHTY.**
FOR **HOLY AND TRUE-**
IS THE ESSENCE OF **BELOVED LIFE REWARDING YOU.**
MARCH 29, 2019

THE GLORY OF THE LORD JESUS, HAS PIERCED THE ONE (SATAN, THE DEVIL) WHO PREVENTS THE NON-BELIEVERS FROM WALKING WITH HIM (CHRIST JESUS)

BARBARA SPEAKING

THE GLORY (CHRIST JESUS)-
YES, HE WHO REIGNS IN THE MIDST OF **HIS HOLY STORY!**
HE HAS PIERCED **THE REALM OF DARKNESS,**
SO THAT THE NON-BELIEVERS MAY **WITNESS HIS GOODNESS.**
FOR **HOLY, HOLY, HOLY-**
IS THE **SAVIOR'S PIERCING GLORY!**
FOR HE HAS **ENTERED THIS DARK REALM AGAIN,**
IN THE FORM OF **BARBARA, HIS SENT MESSENGER AND FRIEND!**
FOR **HOLY AND TRUE-**
IS THE GLORIOUS ONE WHO COMES TO **ME AND BLESSED YOU.**
HE COMES IN THE **FORM OF DIVINE MIGHT-**
AS HIS GLORIOUS PRESENCE PIERCES **THE WORLD'S DARKEST NIGHT.**
FOR **HOLY, HOLY, HOLY-**
IS CHRIST JESUS' HEAVENLY **POWER AND VISIBLE GLORY.**

HOLY AND TRUE-
ARE THE MESSAGES THAT HE SENDS TO ME AND **BLESSED YOU!**
FOR HIS GLORY IS IN **OUR BLESSED MIDST TODAY-**
WITNESS HIM, DEAR ONES, AS YOU SEEK, THROUGH ME, **HIS PIERCING HOLY LIFE SAVING WAY.**
FOR **HOLY AND REAL-**
IS *CHRIST JESUS,* THE HEAVENLY GLORY THAT WE CAN **SEE AND FEEL!**
MARCH 29, 2019

GLORY, GLORY, GLORY

<u>**BARBARA SPEAKING**</u>

GLORY, GLORY, GLORY!
ENTER *CHRIST JESUS,* THE SOVEREIGN KING'S, **LIFE SAVING HOLY STORY!**
FOR **HOLY IS HE** (CHRIST *JESUS*)-
WHO BRINGS HEAVEN'S GOODNESS TO THEE.
GLORIOUS AND RIGHTEOUS-
IS **SOVEREIGN CHRIST *JESUS!***
FOR **HIS GLORY DOES SHINE-**
OVER YOUR **LOVED ONES AND MINE.**
COME AND WITNESS-
THE DIVINE SPLENDOR OF **CHRIST *JESUS*-**
FOR **HOLY AND TRUE-**
IS THE GLORIOUS GOD WHO **SERVES BLESSED AND WORTHY YOU.**
COME AND SEE-
THE GLORY AND DIVINE BRILLIANCE THAT EMIT FROM THE **HOLY BEING OF CHRIST *JESUS*, THE INFINITE ALMIGHTY.**
MARCH 29, 2019

THE SAVIOR: THE GLORY: CHRIST JESUS

BARBARA SPEAKING

CHRIST JESUS, THE SAVIOR OF THIS BLESSED WORLD-
HAS COME TO SHINE HIS GLORY OVER THE SOULS OF THE LIVING BOY AND GIRL.
HE HAS COME, YOU SEE-
IN THE SPIRIT AND ESSENCE OF CHRIST, THE ALMIGHTY.
FOR HOLY AND TRUE-
IS THE SAVING GOD WHO HAS COME TO RESCUE.
HE RESCUES THE STRONG, AND HE RESCUES THE WEAK.
HE RESCUES THOSE WHOM, DIVINE LOVE, THEY DO SEEK.
FOR HOLY AND TRUE-
ARE THEY, WHOM CHRIST JESUS, WILL RESCUE.
MARCH 29, 2019

THE DIVINE TRUTH: THE GLORY: CHRIST JESUS

BARBARA SPEAKING

HE, CHRIST JESUS, IS THE REALM OF DIVINE TRUTH, DEAR ONES.
HE IS THE GLORY AND HEAD OF HIS HEAVENLY AND EARTHLY DAUGHTERS AND SONS.
HE IS REAL, AND HE IS TRUE-
COME, O BLESSED ONES, AND WITNESS THE GLORY (CHRIST JESUS) WHO LOVES CREATED YOU.
FOR HOLY AND REAL-
IS THE GLORY (CHRIST JESUS) THAT YOU CAN REALLY FEEL.
HOLY AND TRUE-
IS THE GLORY THAT CALLS OUT TO YOU.
FOR HEAVEN AND EARTH-
REJOICE AT THE CHOSEN AND BLESSED ONES NEW SPIRITUAL BIRTH.
HOLY, YOU SEE-
IS THE GLORIOUS ONE (CHRIST JESUS) WHO COMES FROM WITHIN BLESSED AND SENT ME.
MARCH 29, 2019

A DIVINE RELATIONSHIP WITH CHRIST JESUS, THE KING OF ENDLESS GLORY

BARBARA SPEAKING

HE (CHRIST JESUS) IS ALL MINE-
FOR HE CALLED AND CHOSE ME, BEFORE THE REALM OF HUMAN MADE TIME.
FOR A DIVINE PERSONAL RELATIONSHIP WITH HE (CHRIST JESUS)-
SEALED THE UNION OF ALMIGHTY GOD AND ME.
HOLY AND TRUE-
DEAR LORD GOD, IS THE PERSONAL RELATIONSHIP THAT MY BLESSED SPIRIT AND SOUL HAS WITH GLORIOUS YOU.
MY BLESSED SPIRIT WILL DANCE WITH YOU-
IN THE MIDST OF THE GLORY THAT IS HOLY, ETERNAL AND TRUE-
FOR OUT OF YOUR DIVINE GOODNESS,
YOU DESCENDED UPON ME WITH YOUR HOLY SPIRIT OF LOVE AND KINDNESS.
HOLY AND TRUE-
IS THE UNBREAKABLE PERSONAL RELATIONSHIP THAT I HAVE WITH BLESSED AND HOLY YOU.
I WILL SHARE OUR HEAVEN DESIGNED LOVE-
WITH THOSE WHOM YOU LEAD, THROUGH ME, TO YOUR HEAVENLY KINGDOM AND HOME ABOVE.
FOR HOLY AND TRUE-
IS THE PERSONAL RELATIONSHIP THAT MY BLESSED SOUL HAS WITH GLORIOUS YOU.
HOLY AND REAL-
IS THE LOVE AND BOND WITH YOU THAT MY SPIRIT AND SOUL FEEL.
MARCH 29, 2019

THE GLORIOUS WORKER OF EVERLASTING MIRACLES: CHRIST JESUS

BARBARA SPEAKING

DESCEND! DESCEND! DESCEND!
ENTER THE OPEN GATES OF BARBARA, YOUR WORTHY AND OBEDIENT EARTHLY FRIEND!
FOR HOLY AND REAL-

ARE THE DESCENDED MIRACLES THAT WE, THE BELIEVING ONES, CAN *SEE AND FEEL.*
FOR *HOLY AND TRUE-*
ARE THE HEAVEN SENT MIRACLES THAT DESCEND EVERY DAY TO *OBEDIENT AND FAITHFUL ME AND YOU.*
RIGHTEOUS, YOU SEE-
ARE THOSE WHO FOLLOW THE DIVINE TEACHINGS AND LOVE OF *CHRIST ALMIGHTY.*
HOLY AND TRUE-
ARE THE MIRACLES AND BLESSINGS THAT *DESCEND TO ME AND YOU!*
MARCH 29, 2019

THE SENT ONE: THE GLORIOUS ONE: *CHRIST JESUS, THE HOLY ETERNAL SON*

CHRIST *JESUS,* THE HOLY ETERNAL SON, SPEAKING

I HAVE BEEN SENT TO YOU, *MY CHILDREN.*
I HAVE BEEN SENT TO LOVE AND BLESS THOSE FROM *EVERY NATION.*
FOR OUR HOLY *GOD AND FATHER ABOVE-*
SENT ME TO REVEAL AND *DELIVER OUR LOVE.*
FOR *HOLY AND REAL-*
IS THE LOVE FOR YOU THAT *GOD, THE FATHER, AND I, TRULY FEEL.*
COME, *O BLESSED ONES!*
SING YOUR SONGS OF GRATITUDE AND PRAISE, O *BLESSED DAUGHTERS AND SONS!*
FOR *HOLY AND TRUE-*
ARE THE LOVE AND GIFTS THAT DESCEND FROM HEAVEN'S OPEN GATES TO *BLESSED AND WORTHY YOU.*
MARCH 29, 2019

THE REDEEMING ONE: THE GLORIOUS ONE: *CHRIST JESUS, THE FATHER'S ONLY BEGOTTEN LIFE SAVING SON*

BARBARA SPEAKING

HE HAS *REDEEMED THE RIGHTEOUS ONES.*

HE HAS SET FREE FROM SIN, *HIS OBEDIENT DAUGHTERS AND SONS.*
FOR *HOLY AND TRUE-*
IS THE HEAVENLY FATHER WHO *REDEEMS BLESSED YOU.*
RIGHTEOUS-
IS *CHRIST JESUS.*
ALL GLORY AND FAME-
SURROUND *HIS ETERNAL LIFE SAVING NAME.*
FOR *HOLY IS HE (CHRIST JESUS)-*
WHO HAS SET *HIS LOVED ONES ON EARTH FREE.*
HOLY AND TRUE-
IS THE GLORY THAT DESCENDS FROM THE GATES OF SWEET HEAVEN FOR *ME AND YOU.*
GLORY, GLORY, GLORY-
SURROUNDS THE BELOVED ESSENCE OF *CHRIST ALMIGHTY.*

BARBARA SPEAKING TO CHRIST JESUS, THE FATHER'S ONLY BEGOTTEN SON

O HOLY ONE (CHRIST JESUS)-
O FAITHFUL AND *ONLY BEGOTTEN SON.*
O HOLY CHRIST JESUS-
I PRAISE AND BLESS YOU FOR *LIVING AMONG SINFUL US.*
MARCH 29, 2019

THE COURAGEOUS ONE: THE HOLY ONE: THE RIGHTEOUS ONE: CHRIST JESUS, THE ALMIGHTY ONE

BARBARA SPEAKING TO CHRIST JESUS, THE ALMIGHTY ONE

O COURAGEOUS ONE-
O HOLY BEGOTTEN SON.
YOU, CHRIST JESUS-
FOUGHT AND WON THE GREAT SPIRITUAL BATTLE FOR **WORTHY US**.
HOLY ARE YOU-
RIGHTEOUS AND GOOD ARE THE THINGS THAT **YOU DO**.
YOU FOUGHT THE DEVIL FOR DEFEATED AND **VULNERABLE US**-
YOU ALONE HAVE THE POWER AND MIGHT THAT WAS GIVEN TO **VICTORIOUS AND ALMIGHTY CHRIST JESUS**.
HOLY AND TRUE-
ARE COURAGEOUS AND **VICTORIOUS YOU**.
YOU ALONE CANE FROM GOD, THE FATHER'S, **HOLY ETERNAL ESSENCE**;
AND YOU ALONE STAND FOREVER MORE IN **HIS RIGHTEOUS AND HOLY PRESENCE**.
HOLY IS HE (JEHOVAH GOD, THE FATHER)-
WHO BEGAT WORTHY AND **OBEDIENT THEE** (CHRIST JESUS).
MARCH 29, 2019

ENTER OUR SINKING WORLD, O GLORIOUS ONE: O HOLY AND ONLY BEGOTTEN SON: CHRIST JESUS

BARBARA SPEAKING TO CHRIST JESUS

ENTER OUR SINKING WORLD, **CHRIST JESUS**.
SEND DOWN THE GLORY THAT WILL **PROTECT AND SHIELD US**.
SEND DOWN **YOUR DIVINE WEAPON OF LOVE**-
SO THAT YOU MAY SHIELD US FROM THE REALM OF EVIL WHO **FEARS OUR COURAGEOUS AND HOLY GOD**.
FOR **UNHOLY IS HE** (SATAN, THE DEVIL)-
WHO **FEARS HOLY THEE**.
FOR **RIGHTEOUS AND TRUE**-
ARE THE HOLY WEAPONS THAT COME FROM **BLESSED AND BELOVED YOU**.

THE REALM OF *EVIL WILL FLEE*-
IN THE HOLY PRESENCE OF *GLORIOUS CHRIST ALMIGHTY*.
SEND OUT *YOUR DIVINE AID*-
TO HELP THE GREAT CREATION THAT *YOU HAVE MADE*.
FOR *HOLY AND TRUE*-
ARE THE EARTHLY FLOCK WHO *SERVES AND FOLLOWS HOLY YOU*.
FREE US, *O HOLY ONE* (CHRIST JESUS)-
RELEASE YOUR CHILDREN FROM WORLDLY SIN AND CAPTIVITY, *O HEAVENLY FATHER'S ONLY BEGOTTEN SON*.
FOR *HOLY AND REAL*-
IS THE GOD WHOM WE CAN *SPIRITUAL SEE AND FEEL*.
MARCH 29, 2019

THE GLORIOUS ONE: THE HOLY ONE: CHRIST JESUS, THE ETERNAL LIVING ONLY BEGOTTEN SON

BARBARA SPEAKING TO CHRIST JESUS, THE ETERNAL LIVING, AND ONLY BEGOTTEN SON

O LIVING ONE (CHRIST JESUS)-

O HOLY AND *ONLY BEGOTTEN SON*-
HOLY AND TRUE-
IS THE FLOCK WHO *FOLLOWS SACRED YOU*.
YOU, O LORD JESUS, ARE THE SOURCE AND *ORIGIN OF THE LIVING*.
FOR YOU, O HOLY ONE, ARE *CHRIST JESUS, THE FORETOLD TRIUMPHANT KING*.
HOLY AND TRUE-
ARE THE SOULS WHO LIVE WITHIN *LIFE SAVING ETERNAL YOU*.
I WILL WEEP-
AS I REJOICE IN THE MIDST OF *MY INTERRUPTED SLEEP*.
FOR THE REALM OF *EVIL AND SIN*-
HAS CAPTURED MY VULNERABLE FAMILY AND *UNSUSPECTING FRIEND*.
O HOLY ONE (CHRIST JESUS)-
O *FATHER'S ONLY BEGOTTEN SON* (CHRIST JESUS).
WEEP WITH ME-
AS I CLING TO THE LOSS AND *FORBIDDEN MEMORY*.

FOR *IT IS REAL*-
THE EVERLASTING TORMENT, IN HELL, *THEY WILL FEEL.*
BUT, *HOLY AND REWARDING*-
ARE THE BLESSED SOULS WHO LIVE IN THE GARDEN OF DIVINE LOVE WITH *CHRIST, OUR VICTORY AND KING.*
MARCH 29, 2019

THE HONORABLE ONE: THE GLORIOUS ONE: CHRIST JESUS, THE PRAISE WORTHY BEGOTTEN SON

BARBARA SPEAKING

HONOR AND PRAISE-
SING THROUGHOUT OUR *REJOICING DAYS!*
FOR *HOLY AND TRUE*-
IS THE GLORIOUS ONE *(ALMIGHTY GOD)* WHO WATCHES OVER *ME AND YOU.*
FOR *HE IS WORTHY*-
HE IS THE RIGHTEOUS AND VICTORIOUS *GOD ALMIGHTY!*
WALK IN THE HOLY *PRESENCE OF CHRIST JESUS,*
AS HE REVEALS HIS GLORY TO *BELIEVING US.*
FOR *HOLY, HOLY, HOLY*-
IS *CHRIST JESUS,* OUR KING OF *ENDLESS LOVE AND GLORY!*
REACH FOR HIS LOVE-
AS HE DESCENDS TO US FROM *SWEET HEAVEN ABOVE!*
FOR *HOLY AND TRUE*-
IS THE WELL OF DIVINE LOVE WHO *DESCENDS TO ME AND BELOVED YOU.*
GIVE HONOR TO *CHRIST, OUR HOLY KING*-
GIVE PRAISE AND HONOR, O BLESSED SPIRITS AS YOU *DANCE AND SING!*
FOR *HOLY AND TRUE*-
IS THE GLORIOUS KING WHO REIGNS OVER *BLESSED ME AND YOU!*
MARCH 29, 2019

BRYAN AND BARBARA ANN MARY MACK

THE GOOD LORD THANKS BRYAN FOR HIS WONDERFUL PRESENCE AND HELP AT THE CHURCH

EPILOGUE

MY GLORY HAS DESCENDED IN YOUR BLESSED MIDST TODAY, DEAR CHILDREN, SAYS CHRIST JESUS, THE LIVING ALMIGHTY GOD AND SAVIOR

BARBARA WITH NICOLE AND HER BEAUTIFUL DAUGHTER

MY OTHER PUBLISHED BOOKS

1. WORDS OF INSPIRATION
2. FATHER, ARE YOU CALLING ME? *(CHILDREN'S BOOK)*
3. DAUGHTER OF COURAGE
4. A HOUSE DIVIDED CANNOT STAND
5. TASTE AND SEE THE GOODNESS OF THE LORD
6. HUMILITY- THE COST OF DISCIPLESHIP
7. WILL YOU BE MY BRIDE FIRST?
8. ODE TO MY BELOVED
9. FATHER, THEY KNOW NOT WHAT THEY DO
10. IN MY FATHER'S HOUSE (CHILDREN'S BOOK)
11. IN MY GARDEN (CHILDREN'S BOOK)
12. THE BATTLE IS OVER
13. THE GOSPEL ACCORDING TO THE LAMB'S BRIDE
14. THE PRESENT TESTAMENT
15. THE PRESENT TESTAMENT VOL. 2
16. THE PRESENT TESTAMENT VOL. 3
17. THE PRESENT TESTAMENT VOL. 4
18. THE PRESENT TESTAMENT VOL. 5
19. THE PRESENT TESTAMENT VOL. 6
20. THE PRESENT TESTAMENT VOL. 7
21. THE PRESENT TESTAMENT VOL. 8
22. THE PRESENT TESTAMENT VOL. 9
23. THE PRESENT TESTAMENT VOL. 10
24. THE PRESENT TESTAMENT VOL. 11
25. THE PRESENT TESTAMENT VOL. 12
26. THE PRESENT TESTAMENT VOL. 13
27. THE PRESENT TESTAMENT VOL. 14
28. THE PRESENT TESTAMENT VOL. 15

29. THE PRESENT TESTAMENT VOL. 16
30. THE PRESENT TESTAMENT VOL. 17
31. BEHOLD THE PRESENT TESTAMENT "VOLUMES 18, 19, 20, 21, 22 AND 23"
32. BEHOLD MY PRESENT TESTAMENT "VOLUMES 24 AND 25"
33. BEHOLD MY PRESENT TESTAMENT "VOLUMES 26, 27, 28 AND 29"
34. BEHOLD MY PRESENT TESTAMENT "VOLUMES 30, 31 AND 32"

CPSIA information can be obtained
at www.ICGtesting.com
Printed in the USA
BVHW022337170419
545845BV00003B/9/P